THE SPIRIT REALM OFFICIAL WORKBOOK
THE PLACE WE WORK WITH GOD IN PRAYER

PATSY CAMENETI

Harrison House

Harrison House P.O. Box 310, Shippensburg, PA 17257-0310

This book and all other Harrison House's books are available at Christian bookstores and distributors worldwide.

For Worldwide Distribution.

Reach us on the Internet: www.harrisonhouse.com.

ISBN 13 TP: 9781667508740

ISBN 13 eBook: 9781667508757

CONTENTS

INTRODUCTION

Welcome to **The Spirit Realm Official Workbook**. This workbook is designed to guide you through a transformative journey, deepening your understanding of the spiritual principles that govern our lives and enhancing your relationship with God. Through a series of chapters, reflective questions, actionable steps, and journaling prompts, this workbook aims to equip you with the tools necessary to navigate the spiritual realm effectively.

Key Takeaways from the Messages

- **Divine Purpose and Prayer**:
- Every believer has a divine purpose. This workbook will help you identify and understand your specific role in God's grand design. Through prayer and meditation, you'll learn how to align your life with His will, recognizing that **God's purposes are intricate and detailed**.
- As you journey through the chapters, you'll see the importance of persistent and focused prayer. Just as

road construction takes time and effort, so does spiritual growth. Prayer assignments are not one-time tasks but ongoing commitments that require dedication and perseverance.

- **The Role of the Holy Spirit:**
- The Holy Spirit is your guide and helper in this journey. He acts as the operations manager, assigning tasks and providing the necessary power and equipment. This workbook emphasizes the need to be sensitive to the Holy Spirit's leading, ensuring that you are always aligned with His direction.
- Understanding the Holy Spirit's role will help you rely more on His guidance, knowing that He calls the workers to their places and equips them for their tasks.
- **Collaboration Within the Body of Christ:**
- God's plans involve many different workers within the Body of Christ. No one can accomplish these plans alone. This workbook highlights the importance of unity and collaboration within the Church. By working together, we can achieve the overarching goal of preparing the way for the Lord's return.
- You'll learn how to engage with others in the Body of Christ, recognizing that each person's role is vital and contributes to the larger purpose.
- **Preparation for the Lord's Return:**
- Just as John the Baptist prepared the way for Jesus' first coming, we are called to prepare the way for His return. This involves bringing down high and proud things, elevating degraded things, and straightening crooked paths in various sectors like government, business, and media.

- The workbook will guide you in identifying areas in your life and community where you can make a difference through prayer and action, ensuring that you are actively contributing to the preparation for the Lord's return.
- **Impact of Persistent Prayer**:
- The workbook emphasizes the power of persistent prayer in transforming societies and influencing nations. You'll see how your prayers can impact governments, businesses, and the media, bringing about God's will on earth as it is in heaven.
- By staying committed to your prayer assignments, you'll be part of a collective effort that prepares the way for God's glory to be revealed to all people.
- **God's Provision for His Purposes**:
- God provides for His purposes. The workbook will help you understand how to trust in God's provision, knowing that He funds His plans and ensures that resources are available when needed. Just as the wise men's gifts were timely for Jesus' family, you'll learn to recognize and rely on divine provision in your life.
- This understanding will build your faith and confidence, knowing that God's provision is always timely and sufficient for His plans.
- **The Convergence of God's Plans**:
- As we approach the fulfillment of God's plans, you'll notice how different aspects of His purposes start to converge and collaborate, creating a powerful movement. The workbook illustrates this through the analogy of gears that used to be far apart now coming together.
- You'll be encouraged to see the bigger picture and how your role fits into the grand scheme of God's

design, contributing to a mighty movement toward the fulfillment of His purposes.

- **The Journey of Faith:**
- The workbook takes you on a journey of faith, emphasizing that every detail in God's plan holds great value. Delighting in these details makes the journey worthwhile, and you'll learn to appreciate each step, no matter how small or insignificant it may seem.
- By reflecting on past experiences and staying committed to your prayer assignments, you'll grow in faith and understanding, recognizing that every prayer and action contributes to God's grand design.
- **Transformative Power of Reflective Questions and Journaling:**
- Reflective questions and journaling prompts are powerful tools for personal growth and spiritual transformation. This workbook encourages you to engage deeply with these exercises, allowing you to explore your thoughts, experiences, and revelations in a meaningful way.
- Through regular reflection and journaling, you'll gain insights into your spiritual journey, identify areas for growth, and celebrate your progress.
- **Encouragement and Hope:**
- Throughout the workbook, you'll find words of encouragement and hope, reminding you that God's plans for you are good and full of purpose. The included Bible verses provide spiritual nourishment and strength, reinforcing the messages and lessons of each chapter.
- By staying connected to these sources of encouragement, you'll be empowered to continue

your journey with confidence and joy, knowing that God is with you every step of the way.

What to Expect from This Workbook

As you work through **The Spirit Realm Official Workbook**, expect to gain a deeper understanding of your role in God's plans and how to effectively navigate the spiritual realm. Each chapter is designed to build upon the previous one, guiding you through a structured and comprehensive journey of spiritual growth.

- **Reflective Questions**: These questions are meant to provoke thought and introspection, helping you to dig deeper into the lessons and apply them to your life.
- **Actionable Steps**: Practical steps are provided to help you implement the lessons in your daily life. These steps are focused on cultivating habits, equipping yourself with knowledge, and engaging with the Body of Christ.
- **Journaling Prompts**: These prompts encourage you to document your journey, capturing your thoughts, experiences, and revelations. This practice not only reinforces the lessons but also serves as a valuable record of your spiritual growth.

By the end of this workbook, you will have a clearer understanding of God's intricate plans and how you fit into them. You will be better equipped to handle ongoing prayer assignments, collaborate with others in the Body of Christ, and contribute to the preparation for the Lord's return. Most importantly, you will grow in faith, trust in God's provision, and experience the joy of being part of His grand design.

INTRODUCTION

May this workbook be a transformative tool in your spiritual journey, helping you to navigate the spirit realm with confidence and purpose. Embrace the journey, delight in the details, and trust that God is working through you to accomplish His glorious plans.

CHAPTER I
AN INVITATION TO WORK WITH GOD

God is not looking for workers who can accomplish tasks on their own strength but for those who are willing to follow His lead and trust His guidance. Your willingness to be led is more valuable than your capacity to lead.

"Abide in Me, and I in you. As the branch cannot bear fruit of itself, unless it abides in the vine, neither can you, unless you abide in Me." - John 15:4, NKJV

One night, I had a dream that really opened my eyes. In this dream, I was shown that sometimes we take on tasks believing they're exactly what God wants us to do. But the truth is, we might have chosen these paths on our own, without a clear nudge from Him. I want to share with you what I learned from this dream, hoping it can help illuminate your path as it did mine.

Understanding Divine Assignment was the first major insight. In my dream, Jesus didn't need my help in a surgery. This was a clear sign that not all my efforts were necessary or even wanted by God. It reminded me that God has specific plans, and not everything I feel compelled to do is part of those plans.

The concept of **'Self-Assignment'** really hit home. I realized that many times I had taken it upon myself to 'help' or intervene without God asking me to. This self-driven action can distract us from truly tuning in to His plans.

When Jesus told me to **Leave the Operating Room**, it meant more than just physically stepping back. It was about mentally and spiritually moving aside, teaching me a powerful lesson about humility and the need to trust God's process without trying to force my own.

Realizing Dependence on God became clearer when I saw that despite my best intentions, they weren't what was needed at that moment. This realization brought home the truth that God's plans do not depend on us, though He invites us to join Him in His work.

Spiritual Pruning for Fruitfulness: Just like gardeners trim plants to help them grow better, God sometimes needs to cut away our unhelpful practices. For me, this meant letting go of unnecessary 'spiritual' tasks that I had imposed on myself.

The dream showed the **Distinction Between Self-effort and Divine Inspiration**. My efforts, no matter how earnest, could not achieve what only God can do. This was a humbling reminder that my true strength comes only from a close relationship with Him.

An **Invitation to Collaborate with God** was revealed to me, urging me to work with Him, not just for Him. This means watching for His guidance at every step and aligning my actions with His will.

The Importance of Spiritual Connection was illustrated through the vine and branches metaphor. Just as a branch draws life from the vine, I was reminded that my spiritual effectiveness comes from my connection to Christ.

Potential of Spirit-led Prayer: There's immense power in prayers that align with God's will. This kind of prayer can move mountains and bring about real change.

Lastly, **Reflecting on Personal Spiritual Practices** encouraged me to examine my prayer life and daily practices to ensure they align with God's desires.

As we continue on this journey, I encourage you to:

REFLECTIVE QUESTIONS

1. Have you ever felt 'self-assigned' to a task or ministry? What were the outcomes?
2. How do you discern between being led by God and operating out of self-effort in your spiritual practices?
3. In what ways have you experienced spiritual pruning, and how has it affected your effectiveness in serving God?
4. What does 'abiding in Christ' look like in your daily life, and how does it influence your prayer life?
5. Can you identify a recent situation where aligning your prayers with God's will led to a noticeable impact?

ACTIONABLE STEPS

- **Cultivate an Attitude of Surrender**: Regularly check and align your intentions with God's will. Let go of self-driven tasks.
- **Equip Yourself with Scriptural Insights**: Deepen your relationship with God through a better

understanding of the Bible. This ensures your actions and prayers are informed by His word.

- **Engage in Reflective Prayer**: Regularly ask for God's guidance on what to embrace and what to let go in your spiritual journey.

JOURNALING **Prompt**

Reflect on a time when you took on a 'self-assigned' role or task. How did it differ from when you engaged in something you felt was divinely guided? What did you learn from both experiences about following God's will?

~

CHAPTER 2
THE MINISTRY OF PRAYER

As you deepen your prayer life, remember that you're not just asking things from God but actively participating in His divine plan. Your prayers are a vital part of His work.

"But without faith it is impossible to please Him, for he who comes to God must believe that He is, and that He is a rewarder of those who diligently seek Him." - Hebrews 11:6, NKJV

L ooking back at my first job in a flower shop at thirteen, I remember working closely with the owners. They taught us about flowers and shared their personal journey to faith. This job wasn't just about arranging bouquets; it was about forming a meaningful connection with those who guided us.

The Value of Workplace Experience showed me the different ways we can relate to our leaders. Some jobs keep us close, like in the flower shop, while others, like my next job as a nurse's aide, position us at a distance. This difference made me see the importance of connecting personally in our roles, especially in spiritual matters.

In the hospital, I followed instructions without ever really knowing who was in charge. **Importance of Relationship in Ministry** struck me; working without a personal relationship felt empty compared to my time in the flower shop.

Understanding Roles within Spiritual Work really opened my eyes. Unlike my time at the hospital, being part of God's kingdom is about having a personal relationship with Jesus. Knowing Him isn't just helpful; it's essential to our work in faith.

Discussing **Working with God vs. Working for God**, I realized effective ministry isn't just about what we do; it's about our relationship with God. This partnership is critical, as highlighted in scriptures like 1 Corinthians 1:9, which calls us into companionship with Jesus.

Scriptural Foundations for Collaboration with God teach us that we're like branches on a vine (John 15:4). We can only be fruitful if we stay connected to Christ, our source.

Reflecting on **The Life of Epaphras as a Model for Prayer Ministry**, I am inspired by his dedication. His prayers strengthened churches and showcased that **Prayer as an Active Service** is a potent form of ministry.

Epaphras' story also highlights **The Power of Aligned Prayer**. When our prayers match God's will, they become incredibly powerful and effective, not just echoing our wishes but fulfilling His plans.

Role of Obedience in Prayer is critical, much like in a surgical team, where everyone must follow the surgeon's lead. Our prayers should align with God's guidance, following His plan rather than our own.

Lastly, **Encouragement to Embrace Prayer Ministry** is for everyone. You don't need a special title to impact others through prayer. Like Epaphras, each of us can have a profound effect on our community and beyond through dedicated prayer.

Let's aim to be more like Epaphras—connected deeply with God, committed to His purposes, and fervent in prayer. Remember, it's not just about presenting our requests; it's about participating actively in God's ongoing work.

REFLECTIVE QUESTIONS

1. How do your current or past job experiences reflect your relationship with God?
2. In what ways can you develop a deeper personal relationship with Jesus?
3. What differences do you find between working with God and working for God in your personal ministry?
4. How can the example of Epaphras inspire your own prayer life?
5. What steps can you take to ensure your prayers are more aligned with God's will?

ACTIONABLE STEPS

- **Cultivate a Prayerful Attitude**: Foster a daily habit of prayer that seeks not just to present requests to God, but to actively engage with His will and purpose.
- **Equip Yourself with Knowledge**: Study the lives of biblical figures like Epaphras who exemplified a powerful prayer life. Understand the principles that made their prayers effective.

- **Engage in Community Prayer**: Join or form prayer groups that focus on interceding for the church and its ministries, aiming to replicate the impactful prayer life of Epaphras.

Journaling Prompt

Reflect on your prayer life. Consider how it compares to that of Epaphras. What aspects of his prayerful dedication can you incorporate into your own practices to make your prayers more aligned with God's will?

～

CHAPTER 3
GOD IS A SPIRIT

As you seek to deepen your connection with God, remember that He is spirit, and those who worship Him must do so in spirit and truth. This journey towards deeper spiritual engagement is not only about seeking answers but about nurturing a relationship with the Divine.

"But the hour is coming, and now is, when the true worshipers will worship the Father in spirit and truth; for the Father is seeking such to worship Him." - John 4:23, NKJV

Have you ever wondered if it's truly possible to work with God, not just for Him? This question has often crossed my mind, especially considering my own experiences where work felt like a routine without any deep connection, similar to my time at the hospital. However, understanding how Jesus interacted with His Father has opened my eyes to what it truly means to collaborate with God in a profound and effective way.

Nature of Working with God—This idea is quite different from the typical job roles we know. Working with God involves more than just doing tasks; it requires a personal connection and understanding of His nature and desires.

Jesus had a unique relationship with His Father, which he spoke about in the scriptures. This relationship allowed Him to work perfectly with God. **Jesus' Understanding of the Father** is something that we, too, can emulate in our spiritual lives to enhance how we serve and connect with God.

The core message that Jesus shared about the Father is that **God is Spirit**. This truth is fundamental but profound. It means that our interactions with Him must transcend our physical senses and occur on a spiritual level. Understanding this helps us see why our prayers and worship must be more than just physical actions or words.

Jesus emphasizes that to truly connect with God, we must **Worship in Spirit and Truth**. This directive isn't just about how we worship but also how we engage with Him in all aspects of our lives, ensuring our interactions are genuine and spiritually aligned.

When our prayers are limited to what we feel or see physically, we miss out on truly connecting with God on a deeper level. **Prayer Beyond the Physical** highlights the importance of engaging with God as a Spirit, which allows us to tap into the full potential of our spiritual practices.

Faith is essential when it comes to receiving from God. It's not just about believing; it's about having a **Faith as a Medium of Reception**—a confidence that what we ask in line with His will, He hears and responds to.

The Bible is the best tool we have to understand God's will. **Scriptural Guidance in Prayer** provides a solid foundation for our prayers, ensuring they are aligned with what God desires to do in and through us.

However, there's a risk in treating our prayers like transactions, just like ordering from a menu. This **Beyond Transactional Prayer** approach encourages us to move past seeing prayer as just asking and receiving, urging us to develop a deeper, more relational engagement with God.

Historically, figures like Adam, Eve, and Enoch show us what it means to have a direct and personal interaction with God. These **Historical Examples of Fellowship with God** not only inspire but also teach us about the opportunities and challenges of such deep relationships.

Finally, this chapter is an **Invitation to Intimate Fellowship** with God. It's an invitation open to anyone who sincerely seeks Him, encouraging us to explore a relationship with God that goes beyond superficial interactions.

As we continue our spiritual journeys, let's aspire to engage with God not just at the surface level but in a way that acknowledges and respects His true nature as a Spirit. This deeper understanding can transform how we live, pray, and worship.

REFLECTIVE QUESTIONS

1. How does understanding God as a Spirit change your approach to prayer and worship?
2. In what ways can you deepen your relationship with God to align more closely with Jesus' example?
3. How do you balance the need for spiritual authenticity with the challenges of daily life in your practice of faith?
4. What steps can you take to move beyond a transactional view of prayer to a more relational engagement with God?

5. How can the examples of Adam, Eve, and Enoch influence your own spiritual practices and relationship with God?

ACTIONABLE STEPS

-   **Cultivate a Spirit-Led Approach**: Practice daily meditations or spiritual exercises that focus on listening and responding to God in a manner that acknowledges His nature as a spirit.
-   **Equip Yourself with Biblical Knowledge**: Regularly study the scriptures that describe how God interacts with His followers, using these insights to guide your prayers and spiritual practices.
-   **Engage in Faith-Driven Prayer**: Deepen your prayer life by consistently praying with faith, seeking to understand and align with God's will rather than your own desires.

JOURNALING **Prompt**

Reflect on your recent spiritual practices. How have you attempted to connect with God as a spirit? What changes can you make to enhance this spiritual engagement and deepen your relationship with Him?

~

CHAPTER 4

COME TO ME

Remember, God's invitation to come into His presence is ever-present and all-encompassing. He calls you to approach with confidence, knowing that through Jesus, you are always welcome into His loving embrace.

"Let us therefore come boldly unto the throne of grace, that we may obtain mercy, and find grace to help in time of need." - Hebrews 4:16, NKJV

I n our songs and prayers, we often call for God to draw near to us. This longing for His presence is a beautiful reflection of our desire to have God in our lives, homes, and communities, similar to the way David and Solomon made extensive preparations to welcome God's presence.

Invitation to God's Presence—it's truly remarkable to consider that as much as we desire God's presence, His wish to be with us is even stronger. God initiated the building of the tabernacle and the system of sacrifices to facilitate His dwelling among His people.

David and Solomon's efforts in constructing the temple demonstrate the importance of preparing ourselves, both spiritually and physically, to welcome God. **David and Solomon's Efforts** teach us about the significance of making space in our lives for God's presence.

The idea that **God's Desire to Dwell Among Us** is shown through His instructions for the tabernacle and His commands for sacrifices. These were not just religious rituals; they were God's way of coming closer to His people.

Jesus' Role in Bridging the Gap explains that Jesus came to earth not just to save us but to make it possible for us to approach God freely and confidently. His mission was to remove the barriers that sin had created between God and humanity.

Scripture encourages us to approach God boldly, trusting in the sacrifice Jesus made. **Scriptural Basis for Approaching God** —verses like Hebrews 10:22 remind us that we can enter God's presence with honest hearts, fully reliant on His mercy.

Universal Invitation—this extends to everyone. Whether you are deeply passionate about your faith or just beginning to explore, God's invitation to draw near is open to all. It's about coming to Him with belief and expectancy.

In this day and age, drawing near to God doesn't require a physical journey but rather a spiritual one. **Shift in Engagement** means turning our focus toward God, recognizing that His presence is all around us, regardless of our physical location.

The chapter also discusses **Practical Ways to Come to God**, which include engaging deeply with His Word, participating in genuine worship, and embracing spiritual disciplines that enhance our connection with Him.

Moreover, how we handle sin and daily worries can either distance us from God or draw us closer, depending on our response. **Impact of Sin and Worries** explores how approaching

God with our failures and anxieties can strengthen our relationship with Him.

Lastly, **Perpetual Open Invitation** emphasizes that God's call to come into His presence is always open, promising not just His nearness but also spiritual rewards for those who seek Him diligently. This continuous invitation is a call to deepen our relationship with God.

REFLECTIVE QUESTIONS

1. How do you personally respond to the invitation to come into God's presence?
2. What can you learn from David and Solomon about preparing your life to be a welcoming place for God?
3. In what ways has understanding Jesus' role in your spiritual life changed how you approach God?
4. How do you handle sin and worries in your life in relation to your relationship with God?
5. What are some practical steps you can take daily to shift your focus and attention towards God?

ACTIONABLE STEPS

- **Cultivate Daily Engagement with Scripture**: Make reading and reflecting on God's Word a daily habit. Expect that God will communicate with you through the scriptures and let this guide your thoughts and actions throughout the day.
- **Equip Yourself Through Worship**: Integrate worship into your daily routine, using music, prayer,

or silent reflection to acknowledge God's presence in your life. This can transform ordinary moments into sacred encounters.

- **Engage in Faithful Reflection**: Regularly assess how you are responding to God's invitation to come closer. Use prayer as a means to confess, give thanks, and seek guidance, thus deepening your spiritual journey.

JOURNALING **Prompt**

Reflect on how you currently respond to God's call to come into His presence. What barriers do you face, and how can you overcome them to foster a closer relationship with God? Consider practical steps you can take to make your daily walk with God more intentional and fulfilling.

~

CHAPTER 5
YOU ARE A SPIRIT

Embrace your identity as a spiritual being designed for communion with God. This relationship is the core of your existence and the source of true fulfillment.

"The Spirit Himself bears witness with our spirit that we are children of God." - Romans 8:16, NKJV

I sn't it amazing to think that God designed us specifically for ongoing communication with Him? This isn't just fascinating—it transforms how we view ourselves and our capabilities. We're not just physical beings; we are created with spirits that can engage directly with God, who is also a Spirit.

Human Design for Divine Interaction—Realizing that we are designed to interact with the divine shows that these connections aren't just possible; they're what we were created for. This design is intentional, crafted so we can have deep connections with the spiritual realm.

Our spiritual capabilities, such as **Capabilities of the Human Spirit**, function like our physical senses but in the spiritual domain. We can spiritually see, hear, and feel, which are crucial for understanding God's will and following His guidance in our lives.

Think about how we physically hunger and thirst for food and water—our spirits also crave spiritual nourishment. **Spiritual Hunger and Thirst** remind us of our deep need for spiritual connection, drawing us closer to God, as described in scriptures like Luke 6:21 and Psalms 42:1-2.

Spiritual Sight and Hearing are not mere metaphors but actual ways our spirit interacts with the divine. Through these senses, we can perceive God's will and hear His directions, helping us navigate our faith and life decisions effectively.

However, it's easy to focus more on our bodies or our intellect, often at the expense of our spiritual nature. **Distracted by the Physical and Intellectual** elements of our existence can overshadow our true spiritual identity, which is vital to recognize and prioritize.

The secret to living a fully realized spiritual life is ensuring that the spirit takes precedence. **Dominance of the Spirit** means living as God intended, fully engaged with Him and the spiritual life He offers.

Being spiritual isn't confined to religious activities; it's about being attuned to the spiritual realm. **Definition of a Spiritual Person** extends beyond regular church attendance—it involves how responsive and aware we are of the spiritual dimensions of our existence.

Throughout history and across various cultures, spirituality has been a common thread. **Universal Spiritual Awareness** demonstrates that people from all backgrounds have engaged with the spiritual realm, though not always in alignment with God's will.

A significant caution in our spiritual engagement is **The Danger of Misdirected Spirituality**. It's possible to be active in the spiritual realm but disconnected from God. It's vital to ensure our spiritual activities align with God's revelations through Jesus Christ.

Finally, **Engagement in True Prayer** is more than routine—it's a dynamic interaction with God where our spirits connect with His purposes. This profound connection is what true prayer and spiritual living are all about.

As we continue on our spiritual journey, let's strive to keep our spirits in charge, guiding us in deeper communion with God. Use your spiritual senses to cultivate a rich, fulfilling relationship with the Creator.

REFLECTIVE QUESTIONS

1. How do you perceive your own spiritual senses working in your daily life?
2. In what ways can you cultivate a stronger spiritual hunger and thirst for God's presence?
3. How might focusing too much on intellectual or physical aspects hinder your spiritual growth?
4. What steps can you take to ensure your spirit remains the dominant part of your being?
5. How can you safeguard your spiritual practices to ensure they are aligned with God's will?

ACTIONABLE STEPS

- **Cultivate Awareness of Spiritual Senses**: Regularly set aside time to engage in spiritual exercises that enhance your awareness of God's presence and voice, such as meditation on scripture or silent prayer.

- **Equip Yourself with Spiritual Knowledge**: Study biblical examples of individuals who exemplified a strong spiritual connection with God. Use these insights to develop your own spiritual practices.
- **Engage in Discerning Prayer**: Be deliberate in your prayer life to seek God's will and align your spiritual activities with His purposes. This involves not just speaking but also listening and responding to God's guidance.

JOURNALING **Prompt**

Reflect on the last time you felt a strong spiritual connection in prayer or worship. What elements contributed to this feeling? How can you incorporate these elements more regularly into your spiritual practice to enhance your connection with God?

∽

CHAPTER 6
HOUSE OF PRAYER

Remember, your body is a temple of the Holy Spirit. Treat it with care, discipline it with love, and use it for God's glory. In doing so, you honor God not just with your spirit and soul, but with your whole being.

"Do you not know that your bodies are temples of the Holy Spirit, who is in you, whom you have received from God? You are not your own; you were bought at a price. Therefore honor God with your bodies." - 1 Corinthians 6:19-20, NKJV

Imagine the rare moments recorded in the Bible when God's voice was heard audibly, like during Saul's dramatic encounter on the way to Damascus, or at Jesus' baptism. These instances are powerful reminders that while God can communicate directly in an audible voice, He often speaks to us through our spiritual senses.

Audible Encounters with God—These exceptional moments show that God can make His voice known in very direct ways. However, for most of us, connecting with God means tuning in spiritually rather than expecting to hear His voice with our ears.

As we grow in our spiritual lives, it's important to realize that our physical bodies can sometimes be a barrier to our spiritual activities. Remember how the disciples struggled to stay awake in the Garden of Gethsemane? Their experience underscores how our physical limitations can interfere with our spiritual intentions.

The Challenge of Physical Limitations—Just as the disciples found it hard to stay awake to pray, we too may find our bodies resistant when we attempt to engage in deep spiritual practices like prayer and fasting. It's not that our bodies are inherently problematic; they just have different needs that can sometimes distract from our spiritual goals.

It's crucial to recognize that our bodies, while susceptible to various influences—including spiritual warfare—are not 'bad.' They are part of God's creation and meant to be valued. Paul reminds us in his letters that our bodies are temples of the Holy Spirit and should be treated with respect.

Our Bodies as Temples—This idea isn't about neglecting the physical but about honoring God through how we care for our physical selves. We are encouraged to discipline our bodies, not as a rejection of them but to ensure they align with our spiritual purposes.

Jesus' ministry and the redemption He achieved through His sacrifice highlight the significance of our physical bodies in God's plan. His suffering was not solely for spiritual salvation but also to affirm the value of our bodies, which are integral to how we worship and serve God.

Redemptive Role of Jesus for Our Bodies—This understanding helps us see our bodies as valuable and worthy of care. By managing our bodies wisely, we enable them to serve effectively in our spiritual lives.

Paul discusses keeping his body under control to prevent it from interfering with his ministry. This kind of discipline is vital for anyone who wishes to lead a spiritually focused life without being hindered by physical desires or limitations.

Discipline and Subjugation of the Body—It's about making sure that our spiritual life is the priority, guiding how we live physically. This doesn't mean ignoring our bodily needs but managing them in a way that supports our spiritual growth.

Our involvement in spiritual activities, like prayer, should be vibrant and active, engaging every aspect of our being—spirit, soul, and body. This comprehensive approach ensures that our spiritual pursuits are supported by our physical actions, not hindered by them.

Active Engagement in Prayer—This involves more than routine practices; it's about making our entire lives a reflection of our spiritual commitments. Each physical action can be an act of worship if it's done with the intention to honor God.

As you reflect on your life, think about how you can better integrate your physical and spiritual practices. Consider your body not just as a vessel or a hindrance but as a vital participant in your spiritual journey.

REFLECTIVE QUESTIONS

1. How can you enhance your spiritual perception to better hear and respond to God?
2. What are some physical habits or practices that might be hindering your spiritual growth?
3. How do you view your body in relation to your spiritual life and ministry?
4. What steps can you take to discipline your body to enhance your spiritual activities?

5. In what ways can you use your physical presence as a 'mobile temple' in your daily life?

- **Cultivate Spiritual Awareness**: Engage in daily practices such as meditation, prayer, and scripture reading to enhance your spiritual senses and reduce the dominance of the physical in your life.
- **Equip Yourself with Knowledge**: Study biblical instances of physical discipline and spiritual engagement to understand how others have successfully managed their physical limitations for spiritual gain.
- **Engage in Holistic Worship**: Incorporate physical acts of worship into your routine, such as fasting, dedicated prayer times, and using your physical presence in acts of service, to honor God with your body.

Journaling **Prompt**

Reflect on the last week: How have you used your body as a temple of the Holy Spirit? What physical activities or disciplines did you engage in that helped or hindered your spiritual connection? Consider what changes you might make to better integrate your physical and spiritual life.

CHAPTER 7
COME TO MOUNT ZION

Embrace your place in Mount Zion, the city of the living God, where you are surrounded by a great cloud of witnesses, angelic beings, and the presence of Jesus Himself. Let this vision lift your spirit and guide your steps in faith.

"But you have come to Mount Zion and to the city of the living God, the heavenly Jerusalem, to an innumerable company of angels, to the general assembly and church of the firstborn who are registered in heaven, to God the Judge of all, to the spirits of just men made perfect, to Jesus the Mediator of the new covenant, and to the blood of sprinkling that speaks better things than that of Abel." - Hebrews 12:22-24, NKJV

Tony and I have traveled to many countries, each with its unique characteristics. Buildings, gardens, and rivers give each city its own look. To truly know a city, though, you have to know the people who live there. The writer of Hebrews 12 helps us understand the spiritual realm where we work with God. He starts by explaining where we are not—Mount Sinai, with its terrifying physical manifestations of God's presence. Instead, we come to a different place—Mount Zion.

Contrast Between Mount Sinai and Mount Zion—Mount Sinai was marked by fire, darkness, and a fearsome voice. It was a place of physical terror. But as believers, we are called to Mount Zion, the heavenly Jerusalem, a place of peace and spiritual connection.

Heavenly Jerusalem—Mount Zion is described as the heavenly Jerusalem, a place filled with countless angels, the spirits of righteous people made perfect, and Jesus Himself. It's a communal and spiritual reality where believers interact with the divine.

Angelic Presence—Angels play a significant role in Mount Zion. They help us understand God's plans, provide protection, and deliver messages. Angels are our fellow servants, but we should focus on God rather than seeking interaction with angels.

Assembly of God's Firstborn Children—This phrase refers to the church, the Body of Christ, which includes believers on earth and in heaven. The unity of the Body of Christ spans both realms, and we work together in God's purposes.

God as Judge and Father—God is both the supreme judge and a loving Father. Coming to Him aligns us with His will and judgment, keeping us in harmony with His purposes.

Mediatorial Role of Jesus—Jesus is central to our interaction with Mount Zion. As the mediator of the new covenant, His presence guarantees the better promises made to God's people, including our redemption and eternal inheritance.

The Sprinkled Blood of Jesus—Jesus' blood speaks of forgiveness and mercy, contrasting with Abel's blood that cried out for vengeance. This highlights the power of Christ's sacrifice in bringing redemption and peace.

Eternal Redemption and Perfecting of Saints—Through

Jesus' blood, even Old Testament saints are made perfect. They are part of the heavenly Jerusalem, cheering on believers still on earth.

Covenantal Blessings through Christ—The new covenant, mediated by Jesus, offers superior promises compared to the old covenant. This covenant is the foundation of our spiritual life and ministry.

Unified Spiritual Endeavor—Mount Zion illustrates a unified spiritual effort involving angels, deceased saints, and living believers. This unity transcends earthly divisions, focusing on collective worship and service to God.

When we work with God in the spirit, we are not alone. We join countless angels in a joyful gathering. These angels assist us in understanding God's plans, providing protection, and delivering messages from God. They are joyful because they are in God's presence, free from fear or sadness. They encourage us to trust in God's presence and help us as we work towards His purposes.

Countless Angels in Joyful Gathering—The presence of countless angels is a reminder that we are not alone in our spiritual journey. Angels assist us and work alongside us in fulfilling God's purposes. They are joyful and provide encouragement, reminding us not to fear.

We are also part of the assembly of God's firstborn children, whose names are written in heaven. This assembly includes the entire Body of Christ, both on earth and in heaven. When we pray, we might be joining others in different parts of the world or even in heaven, united in purpose and prayer.

Assembly of God's Firstborn Children, Whose Names Are Written in Heaven—This assembly refers to the universal church, the Body of Christ, which includes believers on earth and in heaven. Our spiritual work often involves others in the Body of Christ, united in prayer and purpose.

We come to God Himself, who is the judge over all things. Coming to Him aligns us with His will and keeps us on the right path. Just like a musician tunes their instrument to a true pitch, we align ourselves with God to ensure our spiritual activities are in harmony with His purposes.

God Himself, Who Is the Judge Over All Things— Approaching God as the ultimate judge ensures that our spiritual endeavors are aligned with His will. It's essential to keep coming to Him to maintain this alignment.

The spirits of the righteous ones in heaven, who have now been made perfect, are part of this assembly. These saints from the Old Testament and beyond are cheering us on, supporting us as we fulfill our assignments on earth.

The Spirits of the Righteous Ones in Heaven Who Have Now Been Made Perfect—Old Testament saints and other righteous individuals made perfect through Jesus' blood are part of the heavenly assembly, supporting and encouraging believers on earth.

Jesus, the one who mediates the new covenant between God and people, is central to our faith. His role ensures that we have access to the better promises of the new covenant, providing us with the spiritual resources we need.

Jesus, the One Who Mediates the New Covenant Between God and People—Jesus' role as mediator of the new covenant assures us of the better promises and spiritual resources available to believers. His presence is central to our spiritual lives.

The sprinkled blood of Jesus speaks of forgiveness and mercy, unlike Abel's blood, which cried out for vengeance. This powerful image reminds us of the grace and redemption we receive through Christ's sacrifice.

The Sprinkled Blood—The blood of Jesus speaks of forgiveness and mercy, contrasting with Abel's blood that cried out for vengeance. This highlights the grace and redemption available through Christ's sacrifice.

When we come to work with God in the spirit, we do so boldly and humbly. It is a privilege to pray and represent the new covenant, sealed by Jesus' blood. Let us embrace this privilege and fulfill our spiritual roles with dedication and faith.

As we continue on our spiritual journey, let's strive to keep our spirits in charge, guiding us in deeper communion with God. Use your spiritual senses to cultivate a rich, fulfilling relationship with the Creator.

Reflective Questions

1. How does understanding Mount Zion as a spiritual place change your perspective on interacting with God?
2. What role do angels play in your spiritual life according to this chapter, and how does this influence your understanding of God's kingdom?
3. In what ways does the mediator role of Jesus affect your approach to prayer and spiritual engagement?
4. How can the concept of being part of God's 'firstborn children' influence your sense of belonging in the church?
5. What practical steps can you take to more fully embrace the new covenant blessings available through Jesus?

ACTIONABLE STEPS

- **Cultivate a Zion-focused Mindset**: Regularly meditate on the descriptions of Mount Zion and Heavenly Jerusalem to cultivate a spiritual perspective that transcends earthly circumstances.
- **Equip Yourself with Knowledge of Angelic Functions**: Study biblical teachings about angels to better understand their role in God's plan and how they interact with believers.
- **Engage Actively in the New Covenant**: Deepen your understanding of the new covenant through study and reflection, allowing its truths to transform how you live and interact with others in the faith.

JOURNALING **Prompt**

Reflect on your spiritual journey towards Mount Zion. How does this vision of the heavenly Jerusalem influence your daily life, prayers, and interactions with fellow believers? Consider specific ways in which you can live out the reality of being part of this heavenly assembly in your everyday experiences.

∾

CHAPTER 8

THE GATE

Embrace the truth that Jesus is the only gate to the spiritual realm. Trust Him to lead you safely and rightly, knowing He will guide your steps and keep you in His perfect peace.

"I am the gate; whoever enters through me will be saved. They will come in and go out, and find pasture." - John 10:9 NLT

Think about the different rooms in your house. Each room has a specific purpose. For example, the kitchen is where you prepare food, so you'll find appliances like stoves and refrigerators there. You wouldn't expect to find these appliances in a bedroom or bathroom. Similarly, in our spiritual lives, we need to be in the right place to connect with God most effectively, which is the realm of the spirit. Entering this realm is easier than you might think. Just like you enter your house through a door, you enter the spiritual realm through Jesus.

Jesus said, "I tell you the truth, anyone who sneaks over the wall of a sheepfold, rather than going through the gate, must surely be a thief and a robber!" (John 10:1 NLT). This verse tells us that there are other ways to enter the spirit realm, but they are not God's way. Many people from different cultures and religions use various methods to access the spirit realm, such as horoscopes, tarot cards, Ouija boards, and meditation. These methods are like thieves and robbers because they are not the way God provided.

Jesus as the Gate—Jesus Himself described a specific way to access the spirit realm. Getting this right is crucial for a solid prayer life that truly represents God and His will. Jesus has many titles that describe His functions and how we can interact with Him. For instance, "Lamb of God" refers to His sacrificial role, and "Good Shepherd" shows how He cares for us. One important title is "Gate," which indicates that He is the entry point to the spirit realm.

Entering Through Jesus—Jesus said, "I am the gate for the sheep" (John 10:7 NLT). This means there is access through Him. He continued, "Yes, I am the gate. Those who come in through me will be saved. They will come and go freely and will find good pastures" (John 10:9 NLT). This shows that through Jesus, we have free access to the spiritual realm where we find sustenance and guidance.

Avoiding Other Entries—It's important not to be lured by other ways to enter the spirit realm. For us, the only way to enter and engage with the supernatural is through Jesus. The Holy Spirit helps us find the Gate by drawing our attention to Jesus and reminding us of who He is.

Following the Holy Spirit—The Holy Spirit highlights different aspects of Jesus to help us connect with Him. For example, if the Holy Spirit brings to mind Jesus as the "Author and Finisher," we can worship Jesus for being the one who starts and completes our faith. This process helps us enter through the Gate and experience the spiritual realm with Jesus.

Daily Guidance—Every day, the Holy Spirit helps us locate the Gate. While the focus might change, the process of relying on the Holy Spirit to guide us to Jesus remains the same. This guidance brings peace and reassurance, which we can share with others throughout our day.

Dependence on Jesus—No matter how spiritual we become, we will always need Jesus. It's crucial to stay dependent on Him and avoid any spiritual activity that operates independently of Him. Jesus is our example of perfect interaction with the Father, and we should follow His lead.

When you access the spirit realm through Jesus, you can trust that He will guide what you see, hear, and experience. You never have to be afraid because Jesus, the Gate, will lead you in the right direction.

REFLECTIVE QUESTIONS

1. How does viewing Jesus as the Gate change your approach to prayer and entering the spirit realm?
2. What are some ways you can ensure that your spiritual activities are guided by Jesus and not other influences?
3. How can you become more aware of the Holy Spirit's guidance in highlighting different aspects of Jesus to you?
4. What practical steps can you take to remain dependent on Jesus in your spiritual journey?
5. How can you use your experiences with Jesus to encourage and guide others in their faith?

. . .

ACTIONABLE STEPS

- **Cultivate Awareness of Jesus**: Spend time each day reflecting on different titles and aspects of Jesus to deepen your connection with Him as the Gate.
- **Equip Yourself with Scripture**: Study the Bible to understand the various ways Jesus is described and how these titles can help you enter the spirit realm through Him.
- **Engage in Spirit-led Prayer**: Allow the Holy Spirit to guide your prayer time, focusing on Jesus and His role as the Gate to ensure your spiritual activities align with God's will.

JOURNALING **Prompt**

Reflect on a time when you felt especially close to God through prayer or worship. What aspect of Jesus helped you enter the spirit realm during that time? How did the Holy Spirit guide you, and what was the outcome of that experience? Consider how you can apply this experience to your daily spiritual practices.

~

THE GATE

CHAPTER 9
THE STAIRWAY

Embrace the truth that **Jesus is the only stairway** connecting heaven and earth. Through Him, we can ascend to new heights and gain greater visibility and understanding. Trust Him to guide your spiritual journey and deepen your connection with God.

"I tell you the truth, you will all see heaven open and the angels of God going up and down on the Son of Man, the One Who is the stairway between heaven and earth." - John 1:51 NLT

When I was a little girl, my dad would read Bible stories to my siblings and me each night before bed. One of those stories had a picture that left a deep impression on me: a stairway from earth to heaven with angels going up and down. I remember thinking, "This stairway means something special. I wonder what is going on here. Is this stairway real? If so, I'd like to climb it."

Yes, it's true. There really is a stairway from earth to heaven, and the account can be found in Genesis 28. **Jacob sees a ladder in a dream** that connects the seen and unseen worlds.

Jacob was chosen by God for His purposes, but the plan of God for Jacob's life came about in a rather strange way. Typically, the blessing of the father and the family inheritance would go to the firstborn son, but Jacob was not the firstborn. His twin brother Esau was firstborn and should have received that blessing and inheritance. Yet, through deception and favoritism, Jacob received the blessing.

Despite these human flaws, **God's purposes and plans still came to pass**. This challenges our thinking. We often believe that if we do everything right, God's glory will manifest, and His plan will be fulfilled. However, the Bible shows us that even those who fail can still be used by God. King David's moral failures, Samson's weaknesses, and Abraham's mistakes didn't exclude them from God's plan. These stories remind me that God isn't looking for our perfection but for our obedience and responsiveness to Him.

In Jacob's story, he had to run for his life because he made his brother Esau so angry.

"Meanwhile, Jacob left Beersheba and traveled toward Haran. At sundown, he arrived at a good place to set up camp and stopped there for the night. Jacob found a stone to rest his head against and lay down to sleep. As he slept, he dreamed of a stairway that reached from the earth up to heaven. And he saw the angels of God going up and down the stairway. At the top of the stairway stood the Lord, and he said, 'I am the Lord, the God of your grandfather Abraham, and the God of your father, Isaac. The ground you are lying on belongs to you. I am giving it to you and your descendants. Your descendants will be as numerous as the dust of the earth! They will spread out in all directions—to the west and the east, to the north and the south. And all the families of the earth will be blessed through you and your descendants. What's more, I am with you, and I will protect you wherever you go. One day I will bring you back to this land. I will not leave you until I have finished giving you everything I have promised you.' Then Jacob awoke from his sleep and said, 'Surely the Lord is in this place, and I wasn't even aware of it!'" — Genesis 28:10-16 NLT

God reveals His plans to Jacob, plans that were already ordained. **Until this moment, Jacob wasn't aware of God's will** or even God Himself.

Centuries after Jacob's dream, Jesus identifies Himself as the stairway that Jacob saw.

"Then he [Jesus] said, 'I tell you the truth, you will all see heaven open and the angels of God going up and down on the Son of Man, the One Who is the stairway between heaven and earth.'" — John 1:51 NLT

Jesus is the stairway, **the connection between earth and the supernatural realm**. Every step up this stairway gives us more visibility and understanding. We shouldn't stop short but strive to ascend higher.

John and Paul are examples of individuals who ascended this stairway. John was in the spirit on the Lord's Day and had profound spiritual experiences. Paul was caught up in the spirit and saw the spiritual realities of Jesus' finished work. **Their experiences show us the potential of ascending the stairway** and seeing things from a higher perspective.

Whether it's a gate or a stairway, the point is that our access to the unseen spirit realm is through Jesus. **Jesus, only Jesus.**

REFLECTIVE QUESTIONS

1. How does knowing Jesus is the stairway change your perspective on connecting with God?

2. What steps can you take to become more aware of God's presence in your life?
3. How can the stories of Jacob, John, and Paul inspire you to deepen your spiritual journey?
4. What challenges do you face that make you feel unworthy of working with God, and how can you overcome them?
5. How can you rely on Jesus to guide you in your spiritual growth and understanding?

ACTIONABLE STEPS

- **Cultivate Awareness of Jesus:** Reflect daily on Jesus as the stairway to deepen your connection with Him.
- **Equip Yourself with Scripture:** Study the Bible to understand how Jesus is the connection between heaven and earth.
- **Engage in Spirit-led Prayer:** Allow the Holy Spirit to guide your prayer, focusing on Jesus as the way to access the spiritual realm.

JOURNALING Prompt

Reflect on a time when you felt especially close to God through prayer or worship. What aspect of Jesus helped you connect with the spiritual realm during that time? How did the Holy Spirit guide you, and what was the outcome of that experience? Consider how you can apply this experience to your daily spiritual practices.

THE LIVING AND WRITTEN WORD

Embrace the power of **God's Word** and the presence of the Holy Spirit in your life. As you navigate through challenges, remember that God's promises and His teachings are lamps unto your feet, guiding you towards peace and righteousness.

"Your word is a lamp to my feet and a light to my path."
(Psalm 119:105 NKJV)

In Chapter 10, "The Living and Written Word," we explore the profound relationship between the words of Scripture and their living embodiment in Jesus. Imagine God's words as steps on a magnificent stairway that leads us to a higher spiritual understanding. These words are not just sounds or letters; they are spirit and life, perfectly reflecting **God Himself**. They serve as essential tools for understanding the spiritual realm and accessing divine truth.

Understanding **God's will** through these words is crucial because relying solely on our physical senses can lead us astray. The devil is adept at twisting our perceptions in the **natural**

realm, where he thrives by creating confusion and deceit. The Bible, however, provides a clear and unambiguous guide. It reveals God's intentions and heart through the life and teachings of Jesus, **the Living Word**.

However, it's important to recognize that the scriptures can be misused. History shows us that even the most sacred texts can be twisted to justify wrongful actions. This underscores the importance of aligning our understanding with the true nature and teachings of **Jesus**, who perfectly embodies God's Word.

The **Holy Spirit** plays an indispensable role in guiding us through the scriptures. He helps us see beyond the written word to grasp deeper spiritual truths. In prayer, the Holy Spirit often leads us to focus on **promises**, scriptural prayers, praise, and prophecy. These elements strengthen our faith and deepen our connection with God.

God's promises are not just comforting words; they are powerful tools to overcome life's challenges and align us with God's will. These promises enable us to rise above worldly corruption and find spiritual success. By engaging persistently with these promises, we can transform our spiritual journey and gain a deeper experience of **God's presence**, where peace and clarity reign.

This connection through God's Word, aided by the Holy Spirit, not only enriches our spiritual lives but also provides a clear path forward in our daily walk with God. As you reflect on how the scriptures have influenced your life and seek deeper engagement with God's Word, invite the Holy Spirit into your study to unlock its profound truths. Developing a daily practice of engaging with scripture and memorizing passages that resonate with God's promises will equip you with spiritual tools for any challenge.

Remember, God's Word is not just a source of knowledge; it's a lamp to our feet and a light to our path, guiding us through the complexities of life with unwavering truth and light.

Warm regards, [Your Name]

REFLECTIVE QUESTIONS

1. **How do you currently use God's Word in your daily life?** Consider the frequency and depth of your engagement with the Bible.

2. **How can your understanding of the Bible better reflect the character and teachings of Jesus?** Consider whether your interpretation of scripture truly aligns with Jesus' life and teachings.

3. **How do you distinguish between natural influences and spiritual truths when interpreting God's Word?** Think about times when you've struggled to see past the surface and needed deeper insight.

4. **What specific promises from the Bible have you leaned on in tough times?** Assess how these promises have affected your resilience and outlook.

5. **How can you deepen your relationship with the Holy Spirit to enhance your understanding of the scriptures?** Explore ways to invite the Holy Spirit into your daily scripture reading.

ACTIONABLE STEPS

1. **Cultivate**: Develop a daily practice of engaging with God's Word, focusing on scriptures that enhance your

understanding of His promises and aligning your actions with His teachings.

2. **Equip**: Memorize scriptures that resonate with God's promises and teachings, making them a ready tool for times of need and reflection.

3. **Engage**: Regularly invite the Holy Spirit into your study of the Word, seeking His guidance to unlock deeper meanings and applications that align with God's will.

Journaling **Prompt**

Reflect on a recent challenge you faced. Write about how you sought God's guidance through His Word and the outcome. Consider what you learned about relying on God's promises and how this experience has strengthened your faith.

～

CHAPTER 11
PRAYER AND PRAISE

Always remember, the most significant movements in our lives begin not in our busy efforts, but in quiet moments of connection with God. It's not by our might, nor by our power, but by His Spirit that we find true strength and resolution.

"And the Lord said to Paul one night in a vision, 'Do not be afraid, but speak, and do not keep silent; for I am with you, and no one will attack you to hurt you; for I have many people in this city.'" (Acts 18:9-10, NKJV)

I n this chapter, I want to share how deeply prayer and praise have touched my life, especially through the apostle Paul's prayers and the powerful role of praise as we see in the Scriptures.

When my sister and I first discovered **Paul's prayers** in his letters to the early churches, it was a game-changer. These aren't just ordinary prayers; they're profound, aiming to deepen our spiritual connection. They ask for things so lofty, things we might not think to ask for, which can transform us in powerful ways.

I've learned that **praying these prayers** has elevated me spiritually. I've gained new perspectives, accessed deeper insights, and felt closer to God. It's like climbing to a lookout where everything below looks different and more meaningful.

Paul's prayers were not made up on the spot; they came from his deep spiritual encounters with God. This shows us that our prayers should stem from a **deep connection with God**, not just recited from memory.

The New Testament letters are packed with prayers that can guide our own prayer lives. These prayers are not just formalities but are potent words meant to **draw us closer to God**. I encourage you to explore them and let them shape your prayer approach.

Think about the story from **2 Chronicles 20**. The Israelites were surrounded by enemies, a seemingly hopeless situation. Instead of succumbing to fear, they praised God, which changed their outlook and led to a miraculous victory. This story always reminds me to focus on God's greatness instead of my problems.

Like the Israelites, **Paul and Silas** faced their own grim situation in prison. Yet, their worship opened the way for God's power, which freed them through an earthquake. This shows us that no matter our circumstances, worship can lead to freedom.

Praise is more than just a pleasant activity; it's a **spiritual tool**. It changes our atmosphere, shifts our focus from despair to hope, and invites God's intervention. Whenever I'm faced with challenges, I turn up my praise because it reaffirms that God is bigger than any issue.

It's essential not just to pray but to pray **in God's presence**. This involves starting with thanksgiving and moving into deep praise, which draws us closer to Him and paves the way for His supernatural work in our lives.

I once helped a young woman, deeply hurt by her past, find healing by bringing her into God's presence. This wasn't about having all the answers but about connecting her to the One who does. It's a powerful lesson in the **impact of spiritual guidance**.

Whenever I'm immersed in the spirit through prayer, I discover new insights into Scripture relevant to my needs. It's like God lights up a path, showing me the way forward not just with knowledge, but with **wisdom** that directly applies to my life.

REFLECTIVE QUESTIONS

1. How do you currently use the prayers of Paul in your prayer life? Do you see them as merely historical texts, or do you actively seek to understand and utilize them in your spiritual journey?
2. Can you recall a time when praise or worship significantly changed your perspective or situation? What does this tell you about the power of praise?
3. Reflect on a moment when you felt truly in God's presence during prayer. What were the circumstances, and how did it change your outlook or situation?
4. How can you incorporate more scripture and divine inspiration into your daily prayers to make them more effective and aligned with God's will?
5. In what ways can you help others experience the power of God's presence, as I did with the young lady from Rhema?

ACTIONABLE STEPS

- **Cultivate a Habit of Praise**: Begin each day by listing five things you are grateful for. This simple act of gratitude shifts your focus from the problems you face to the blessings around you, enriching your spiritual perspective.
- **Equip Yourself with Scripture**: Take time each month to memorize one of Paul's prayers. Let these words live in your heart and guide your prayers, allowing the Holy Spirit to deepen your connection with God through Scripture.
- **Engage in Spiritual Mentorship**: Consider leading a prayer group or mentoring someone in your community. Use the insights from this chapter to enrich your sessions, focusing on how we can all access the spiritual realm through heartfelt prayer and genuine praise.

JOURNALING **Prompt**

Reflect on a recent challenge or problem you faced. Write about how changing your perspective through prayer and praise might alter the outcome. Consider how you can apply the principles of spiritual ascension to gain a divine perspective on other areas of your life.

∾

CHAPTER 12
PROPHECIES

Remember, the purpose of prophecy is not to awe us with foreknowledge, but to align us more closely with God's eternal purposes. Lean into these divine insights as they are meant to guide, protect, and motivate us towards spiritual maturity and effectiveness.

"But the word of the Lord endures forever." (1 Peter 1:25, NKJV)

In this chapter, I explore how prophecies aren't just forecasts about what's to come; they are pathways that lead us deeper into the spiritual realm. Through engaging with prophecy, we can gain incredible insights and see beyond our usual understanding of time and space.

Prophecies, like those we find in the Bible, can seem overwhelming at first, but they play a crucial role in deepening our spiritual awareness. Take for example **Daniel's Engagement with Prophecy**. Daniel didn't just read words; he actively used

Jeremiah's prophecy to connect deeply with God, which led him to profound spiritual experiences.

It's quite remarkable how, when Daniel began to pray based on the prophecy, there was an **Immediate Response to Prayer**. This response wasn't ordinary; an angel, Gabriel, came swiftly to provide Daniel with further insights. This shows how closely heaven listens when our prayers align with God's prophetic words.

In the spiritual realm, **Timelessness** is a fundamental aspect. Here, the past, present, and future merge, allowing us to see God's plans unfold without the usual constraints of time. This is where prophecies excel, as they offer glimpses into the broad scope of God's eternal purposes.

When Daniel shifted his focus from his physical circumstances in Babylon to a spiritual viewpoint, he illustrated the **Shift from the Natural to the Spiritual**. This shift is crucial for us as believers because it moves our focus from earthly troubles to heavenly insights.

One of the most exciting parts of engaging with prophecies is realizing the **Purpose and Detail in God's Plan**. Unlike the often chaotic and confusing details we encounter in the natural world, the spiritual realm lays out God's purposes with clarity and precision.

Prophecy as a Tool for Spiritual Warfare is another powerful aspect of prophecies. They aren't just for gaining knowledge; they equip us for spiritual battles, providing strategies and encouragement directly from God. This is how prophecies can empower us, similar to how Paul encouraged Timothy to use prophetic words to wage good spiritual warfare.

Re-articulating prophecies, or **Re-articulation of Prophecies**, does more than just echo what has been said; it activates and reaffirms God's promises. This not only strengthens our faith but also propels the fulfillment of God's plans.

Finally, the **Collaborative Nature of Prophecy** is truly inspiring. Prophecies often involve a collective element, where believers from different times and places unite in spirit to bring God's plans to fruition. This unity is a powerful testament to the living nature of God's word.

Through prophecies, we're not just reading or hearing about God's plans—we're actively participating in them. This engagement is essential for our spiritual growth and for fulfilling the roles God has designed for us in His grand narrative.

REFLECTIVE QUESTIONS

1. How do you personally react to biblical prophecies? Do you see them as relevant to your current spiritual journey?
2. Have you ever experienced a moment when a prophecy provided clarity or direction in your life? How did that change your perspective or actions?
3. What steps can you take to incorporate a more active engagement with prophecy in your prayer life?
4. How does the concept of the timelessness of the spiritual realm affect your understanding of God's operations in your life and history?
5. In what ways can you use prophecy as a tool in your own spiritual battles?

ACTIONABLE STEPS

- **Cultivate an Understanding of Prophecy**: Start by studying key biblical prophecies and their fulfillments. This will help you recognize the depth and accuracy of God's Word and how it unfolds in human history.

- **Equip Yourself with Prophetic Scriptures**: Memorize scriptures that contain prophecies which resonate with your spiritual journey. This equipping will prepare you to use these words in times of need, both for encouragement and spiritual warfare.
- **Engage in Prophetic Prayer**: Regularly incorporate specific biblical prophecies into your prayers. Pray for their fulfillment according to God's timing and purposes, thus aligning your prayers more closely with God's overarching plans.

JOURNALING **Prompt**

Reflect on a prophecy from Scripture that has significant meaning for you. Journal about how this prophecy could be influencing your life currently and how it might shape your future actions and decisions. Consider the ways in which this prophecy connects you with believers across different times and places.

∽

PROPHECIES

CHAPTER 13

THE SPIRIT REALM

Remember, no matter where you are physically, you are free in the Spirit. God has equipped you to transcend your physical limitations and engage with Him on a spiritual level that changes both your reality and that of those around you.

"For we walk by faith, not by sight." (2 Corinthians 5:7, NKJV)

I n this chapter, I want to explore how, as believers, we're not confined by our physical circumstances. Through my experiences and the biblical story of John on the island of Patmos, we can see that our spiritual lives can extend far beyond our physical locations.

During the COVID-19 lockdowns, when physical travel was halted, I discovered a profound truth: spiritually, I could go anywhere. This wasn't just a comforting thought; it became a vivid reality as I engaged in prayer and spiritual warfare, reaching as far as Europe, the Middle East, and North America. This ability to transcend physical barriers shows that we are

Unbound by Physical Limits and can participate in God's work from anywhere, at any time.

Consider the Apostle John, exiled to the remote island of Patmos as a form of punishment and isolation. However, instead of being silenced, John received the profound visions that would become the Book of Revelation. This demonstrates that like John, we are **never, ever bound to our physical location** if we know how to engage in the spirit.

Facing challenges or feeling isolated can make it easy to focus on our problems and constraints. However, maintaining a **Spiritual vs. Physical Focus** is crucial. John could have sunk into self-pity or bitterness due to his unfair treatment and harsh conditions. Instead, he chose to focus on his spiritual mission, which led to receiving significant revelations from God.

The Dangers of Self-Pity and Offense can derail us from our spiritual paths. John avoided these pitfalls. He didn't waste his time feeling sorry for himself or holding grudges against those who had wronged him. By focusing on spiritual realities, he was able to transcend his physical imprisonment.

Engaging in the Spirit Realm involves more than just passive belief; it requires active participation in spiritual practices such as prayer, worship, and meditation. These practices open us up to God's presence and empower us to act effectively against spiritual opposition.

In the spirit realm, our awareness shifts significantly. We become acutely aware of God's presence, His will, and our role in His plans. **Visibility and Awareness in the Spirit** are akin to being in a room where you are fully aware of your surroundings. This heightened awareness enables us to pray more effectively and understand God's guidance clearly.

The Influence of the Spirit Realm is profound. John's spiritual revelations on Patmos have influenced Christian theology for millennia, showing that our spiritual contributions can have long-lasting impacts, far beyond what we might expect from our physical locations.

Potential Unlocked in the Spirit speaks to the empowerment we experience in the spirit realm. Here, we tap into our true strength and calling, far removed from earthly limitations. This potential grows as we learn to dwell more in the spirit.

The Immediate Accessibility of the Spirit Realm is an empowering truth. We don't need to travel or wait for the right conditions to access the spiritual. It's available immediately, wherever we are, through faith and spiritual discipline.

Lastly, **Living in the Spirit** should be our goal as believers. This doesn't just mean occasional spiritual experiences but making the spirit realm the base from which we approach our daily lives. It's about maintaining a constant spiritual perspective and letting that guide our actions and decisions.

REFLECTIVE QUESTIONS

1. How often do you feel limited by your physical circumstances? How can understanding your access to the spirit realm change your perspective?
2. Reflect on a time when focusing on spiritual truths helped you overcome a challenging situation. What did you learn from that experience?
3. What practical steps can you take to reduce the influence of negative emotions like self-pity and offense in your spiritual life?
4. How can you cultivate a greater awareness of the spirit realm in your daily life?
5. What does it mean to you to live in the spirit? How can this be reflected in your daily actions and decisions?

· · ·

ACTIONABLE STEPS

- **Cultivate Awareness of the Spirit**: Practice mindfulness of God's presence throughout your day. Start with setting specific times for prayer and meditation, focusing on sensing the Holy Spirit's presence.
- **Equip Yourself with Spiritual Disciplines**: Develop a routine that includes reading the Word, prayer, fasting, and other spiritual disciplines. These practices open doors to deeper spiritual experiences and insights.
- **Engage Continuously with the Spirit**: Make it a goal to engage with the spirit realm daily. Use what you learn from the scriptures and spiritual leaders to maintain a heavenly perspective, even in earthly matters.

JOURNALING **Prompt**

Journal about a recent situation where you felt limited or confined. Reflect on how engaging more deeply in the spirit could alter your perspective and outcome. Write about steps you can take to become more spiritually aware and active, even when physically constrained.

∾

CHAPTER 14

SEEING AND HEARING IN THE SPIRIT

Remember, the realm of the spirit is not a distant or inaccessible place. It's a dimension of reality that you are invited to explore and experience. God is always speaking and showing things to His children. It's up to us to tune in and respond.

"The Lord is near to all who call upon Him, to all who call upon Him in truth." (Psalm 145:18, NKJV)

I n this chapter, I delve into how we can see and hear in the spirit, much like John did in the Book of Revelation. This isn't about using our physical senses; it's about tuning into the spiritual realm where God communicates directly with us.

John's experience on the Lord's Day is a perfect example. While exiled on the island of Patmos, he wasn't just sitting around. He was engaged in deep worship, and it was during this time he heard a voice like a trumpet and saw visions of Jesus. This wasn't with his physical ears or eyes—John was using his **spiritual senses**. From this experience, he received clear instructions to write what he saw and send it to the seven churches.

These events teach us that **spiritual perception** is not confined by our physical limitations. We, too, can receive clear, direct communication from God. This is crucial because it demonstrates that spiritual messages can be as specific and detailed as physical ones, providing deep insights into spiritual truths.

Furthermore, John's visions demonstrate the **detailed spiritual visions** one can have. He described Jesus with intense detail —His robe, the gold sash, His white hair, eyes like flames of fire, and more. This vivid imagery tells us that visions in the spirit can be incredibly rich and informative.

A key lesson we learn from John is the **separation from worldly influences**. While in the spirit, John was cut off from the noise of the world—the politics, the news, the fears. He was wholly focused on the divine revelation being given to him. This teaches us the value of disconnecting from our worldly concerns to fully engage with spiritual messages.

John's experience also highlights the **exclusivity of spiritual content**. In the spirit, he didn't hear complaints or defeat; he heard the empowering and eternal words of Jesus. This reminds us that in the spirit, the communication is pure and focused solely on God's message.

This level of engagement also brought **emotional stability in the spirit** for John. Despite being in a potentially terrifying situation, exiled and isolated, John was calm and focused enough to receive and comprehend these complex visions. This shows us that being in the spirit can stabilize our emotions, overshadowing our fears and concerns with the presence of God.

Moreover, seeing Jesus in such majesty reinforced John's understanding of **spiritual authority**. Jesus, holding the keys of death and the grave, demonstrated His ultimate authority over life and death, a comforting reminder of Christ's power and our security in Him.

John's writings from Patmos, especially the Book of Revelation, illustrate the **impact of spiritual revelations**. What he received in the spirit has shaped Christian thought for centuries, showing us the significant impact our spiritual experiences can have.

These experiences are not just for the likes of John but are accessible to all believers. This **accessibility of the spirit realm** means that anyone can tune into God's frequency, hear His voice, and see His visions, no matter where they are or what situation they find themselves in.

Lastly, we are encouraged to not just visit but to **live in the spirit**. This means making our spiritual engagement continuous, letting it influence our daily lives and decisions. Living in the spirit transforms how we interact with the world, making us more aware of God's kingdom and less influenced by worldly troubles.

REFLECTIVE QUESTIONS

1. How often do you engage in activities that enhance your spiritual senses, such as prayer or worship?
2. Can you recall a time when you felt you received a clear message or direction from God? What impact did it have on your life?
3. In what ways can you minimize distractions to better hear and see in the spirit?
4. How do the descriptions of Jesus in Revelation shape your understanding of His nature and authority?
5. What changes might you need to make in your life to be more receptive to spiritual revelations?

ACTIONABLE STEPS

- **Cultivate Spiritual Sensitivity**: Regularly set aside time for silence and solitude to practice listening and seeing in the spirit. This can involve meditative reading of scriptures, especially those describing spiritual visions like in Revelation.
- **Equip Yourself with Knowledge**: Study biblical examples of spiritual encounters to understand the context, significance, and outcomes of these events. This will help you recognize and appreciate when you might be having spiritual experiences.
- **Engage in Spiritual Disciplines**: Incorporate disciplines such as fasting, prayer, and worship into your routine to enhance your spiritual receptivity. These practices can clear mental and emotional clutter, making it easier to enter into the spirit.

JOURNALING **Prompt**

Reflect on your current spiritual practices and consider whether they are helping you to see and hear in the spirit. Journal about any moments where you felt a spiritual insight or communication. What was the context, and how did it affect you? What can you do to foster more of these moments?

CHAPTER 15

PROPHETIC PRAYER

Remember, engaging in prophetic prayer is not just about speaking to God; it's about listening to Him and allowing His Spirit to guide your words and actions. As you grow in this area, you'll find your prayer life becoming more dynamic and impactful.

"But you, beloved, building yourselves up on your most holy faith, praying in the Holy Spirit." (Jude 1:20, NKJV)

In this chapter, I explore the profound impact that learning from the Old Testament prophets has had on my understanding of prophetic prayer. Unlike routine prayers, **prophetic prayer** is deeply connected to spiritual insights revealed in the moment.

The prophets were uniquely equipped to understand **God's plans and purposes**. They didn't just pray out of routine—they prayed in response to specific visions and messages they received from God. This type of prayer is known as prophetic because it flows from these divine revelations, not from our own desires or the immediate circumstances around us.

Every believer who learns to work with God in the spirit has the opportunity to help bring about **God's purposes** on Earth through prophetic prayer. It's incredible to see how we can serve as conduits for God's plans, helping to manifest His will in the world.

Prophetic prayer is characterized by its spontaneity and its inspiration from God. It's not pre-planned or based on our personal thoughts. It arises spontaneously, guided by the **Holy Spirit**. Think of it as catching a spark from the Holy Spirit and letting that inspiration guide your prayers and actions.

Paul emphasizes this in 1 Corinthians 14, where he encourages all believers to seek the gift of prophecy. He explains that prophetic words can reveal deep truths that open people's hearts to God's presence. This type of prayer has the power to **uncover hidden truths** and lead people to recognize God's work among them.

True prophetic prayer is always spontaneous and relies entirely on the Holy Spirit for direction. It's not scripted. It comes alive as we listen to God and respond to His revelations. This might seem daunting at first, but it becomes more natural over time, like learning to ride a bike. And remember, just as you can't steer a parked car, you can't steer a prayer that isn't moving. Being spiritually active keeps you ready to follow where the Spirit leads.

I once learned a crucial lesson about following the right lead. My husband, Tony, and I accidentally followed the wrong car, thinking it was our friend leading us to a restaurant. We ended up in the wrong place and led others astray as well. This experience taught me the importance of making sure we're following **God's direction** and not just going along with someone else's path, especially in our spiritual lives.

If you simply mimic someone else's prayer style or if you're more attuned to others than to the Spirit's guidance, your prayer life may veer off course. You must discover your unique path in prayer, which comes from being sensitive to the **Holy Spirit's promptings**.

There is something truly remarkable about being in a group where everyone is attuned to the Holy Spirit's guidance. It's like being part of an orchestra where the Holy Spirit is the conductor, and everyone's contributions harmonize under His direction.

In prophetic prayer, you might sometimes see immediate, dramatic results, or you may never know the full impact of your prayers until heaven. But the primary reason to respond to God's prompts is to obey Him. Responding to His guidance is an act of love and worship, as Jesus said.

Prophetic prayer isn't just about asking for things; it's about aligning ourselves with God and declaring His will on Earth as it is in heaven. It's a dynamic, living way to interact with God and to participate actively in His divine purposes.

REFLECTIVE QUESTIONS

1. How often do you engage in activities that enhance your spiritual senses, such as prayer or worship?
2. Can you recall a time when you felt you received a clear message or direction from God? What impact did it have on your life?
3. In what ways can you minimize distractions to better hear and see in the spirit?
4. How do the descriptions of Jesus in Revelation shape your understanding of His nature and authority?
5. What changes might you need to make in your life to be more receptive to spiritual revelations?

. . .

ACTIONABLE STEPS

- **Cultivate Spiritual Sensitivity**: Regularly set aside time for silence and solitude to practice listening and seeing in the spirit. This can involve meditative reading of scriptures, especially those describing spiritual visions like in Revelation.
- **Equip Yourself with Knowledge**: Study biblical examples of spiritual encounters to understand the context, significance, and outcomes of these events. This will help you recognize and appreciate when you might be having spiritual experiences.
- **Engage in Spiritual Disciplines**: Incorporate disciplines such as fasting, prayer, and worship into your routine to enhance your spiritual receptivity. These practices can clear mental and emotional clutter, making it easier to enter into the spirit.

JOURNALING **Prompt**

Reflect on your current approach to prayer. How often do you seek to listen for God's voice as opposed to only presenting your requests? Journal about any specific times when you felt led by the Holy Spirit in prayer and the outcomes of those prayers. What changes can you make to be more open to prophetic prayer?

~

PROPHETIC PRAYER

CHAPTER 16

TENDER COMPASSION

Remember, engaging in compassionate actions is not just about feeling empathy; it's about allowing God's love to move you to help those in need, reflecting His perfect love through your actions.

"But you, beloved, building yourselves up on your most holy faith, praying in the Holy Spirit." (Jude 1:20, NKJV)

I n this chapter, I explore one of the most profound aspects of working with God: compassion. Compassion isn't just a word we hear often; it's a deep, meaningful expression of God's love that might not be fully understood in everyday life. The Bible offers extensive guidance on how to understand and practice **compassion effectively**.

I've deliberately used the word "tender" in previous chapters to highlight a specific aspect of compassion. This term has helped me appreciate how **God's perfect love** manifests as tenderness towards people. When you walk and work closely with the Lord, you'll experience a tenderness that reflects not your own goodness but God's incredible love and kindness.

Psalm 86:15 describes God as full of compassion and mercy, slow to anger, and abundant in love and truth. God's compassion isn't about irritation or dismissal; it's about deep, abiding love that **sees and responds to the pain** in others.

Jesus perfectly modeled this compassion. For instance, when He saw the crowds, He didn't just feel sorry for them; He was **moved to act**, healing their sick and teaching them because He felt their needs acutely. This kind of response—being moved to act because of the suffering of others—is at the heart of true compassion.

Compassion was behind many miracles. It wasn't pity that moved Jesus; it was genuine empathy and love that compelled Him to heal the blind and the sick. Even His teachings were driven by compassion, aiming to fill the gaps in people's understanding, not to showcase His own knowledge.

The story of the Good Samaritan is a classic example of **compassion in action**. Unlike the priest and the Levite in the story, the Samaritan didn't ignore the beaten man; he was moved by compassion to help him. This story challenges us to consider how we respond to the suffering around us.

However, there's a crucial difference between sympathy and compassion. Sympathy might lead us to feel sorry for someone, but it doesn't necessarily move us to help. Compassion, on the other hand, is about being moved so deeply by someone's pain that we're compelled to help change their situation.

For example, when Jesus multiplied the loaves and fish, it wasn't just to perform a miracle. He saw that the people were hungry and His compassion moved Him to feed them. This miracle started from a place of **tenderness and caring** for the needs of the people around Him.

It's important that we don't just sympathize from a distance or get caught up in feeling sorry for others without taking action. True compassion drives us to engage actively and to make a real difference. It involves **feeling with someone** and then stepping in to help, guided by God's love and power.

As we grow in our faith and walk with God, developing a compassionate heart is key. It's not just about feeling; it's about doing. It's about letting God's love flow through us to others, particularly those who are hurting or in need. As we align ourselves with God's heart, our lives and actions can become powerful testimonies of His love and compassion in the world.

REFLECTIVE QUESTIONS

1. How often do you engage in activities that enhance your spiritual senses, such as prayer or worship?
2. Can you recall a time when you felt you received a clear message or direction from God? What impact did it have on your life?
3. In what ways can you minimize distractions to better hear and see in the spirit?
4. How do the descriptions of Jesus in Revelation shape your understanding of His nature and authority?
5. What changes might you need to make in your life to be more receptive to spiritual revelations?

ACTIONABLE STEPS

- **Cultivate Spiritual Sensitivity**: Regularly set aside time for silence and solitude to practice listening and seeing in the spirit. This can involve meditative reading of scriptures, especially those describing spiritual visions like in Revelation.

- **Equip Yourself with Knowledge**: Study biblical examples of spiritual encounters to understand the context, significance, and outcomes of these events. This will help you recognize and appreciate when you might be having spiritual experiences.
- **Engage in Spiritual Disciplines**: Incorporate disciplines such as fasting, prayer, and worship into your routine to enhance your spiritual receptivity. These practices can clear mental and emotional clutter, making it easier to enter into the spirit.

Journaling Prompt

Reflect on your current approach to prayer. How often do you seek to listen for God's voice as opposed to only presenting your requests? Journal about any specific times when you felt led by the Holy Spirit in prayer and the outcomes of those prayers. What changes can you make to be more open to prophetic prayer?

∾

CHAPTER 17

THE ROCK

Remember, engaging with God as the Rock is not just about
acknowledging His power; it's about finding stability and
security in His eternal nature. Trust in Him, for He is unchanging
and reliable.

**"Trust in the Lord always, for the Lord God is the eternal
Rock." (Isaiah 26:4, NKJV)**

I n this chapter, I want to share how understanding Jesus as
the Rock has deepened my faith and trust in God. This isn't
just a metaphor; it's a powerful description of God's
unchanging and eternal nature, which provides a solid foundation for our lives.

The Bible often refers to God as our Rock. This concept is
vividly illustrated in Isaiah 26:4, which tells us to trust in the
Lord always, for He is the eternal Rock. The Hebrew word for
"eternal" here, *olam*, means long duration, antiquity, and futu-
rity—emphasizing God's timeless nature. Just like the Rocky

Mountains in Colorado, which remain steadfast despite the changing world around them, **God remains constant**.

Throughout my life, I've observed many changes—political, cultural, and more. Yet, every time I return to Colorado, the mountains are just as I remember them. They are unaltered by time or circumstance. This stability in nature mirrors the steadfastness of God. While wooden structures in those mountains may deteriorate, the stone buildings in places like Italy, built centuries ago, still stand strong. This durability of rock is an apt metaphor for **God's enduring presence** in our lives.

In the book of Revelation, Jesus describes Himself with terms that speak to His eternal role and nature, like alpha and omega, beginning and end, first and last. These aren't just titles; they are profound truths about who He is. Jesus emphasizes these aspects of Himself to highlight the significance of His eternal nature. When He repeats these descriptions, it's not from forgetfulness but to underscore their importance.

Understanding Jesus as both the beginning and the end, the first and the last, is crucial for us. It means that He encompasses all of time and existence. This understanding gives us access to eternal truths, allowing us to see beyond the immediate and transient, to grasp the enduring truths of God.

Moreover, the world is full of misinformation and lies, especially about our pasts and futures. The devil often uses half-truths to deceive and lead people astray. However, in the spirit, connected with Jesus, our eternal Rock, we are exposed to the truth—the truth that liberates and guides. Whether it's recalling a biblical event to encourage us or understanding our personal pasts, being in tune with Jesus gives us clarity and insight.

People often seek knowledge and understanding through means like horoscopes or tarot cards, driven by a desire to grasp the unknowable. Yet, these practices can lead to deception and bondage. True wisdom and knowledge come only through Jesus, who is the truth. Attempting to gain spiritual insight without Him leads us into dangerous territory.

Jesus, the Author and Finisher of our faith, reminds us that He not only initiates our faith journey but also brings it to completion. This idea is symbolized by a circle, where the beginning and end are connected. Just as Jesus is both the beginning and the end, He is involved in every aspect of our faith journey, from start to finish.

In Isaiah 46:10, God declares that He makes known the end from the beginning. This foreknowledge isn't just about showing off divine power—it's about providing assurance and security for us. Knowing that God has a purpose and that He will accomplish what He pleases should give us great comfort and confidence as we live our lives based on His eternal truths.

REFLECTIVE QUESTIONS

1. How does understanding God as the eternal Rock influence your trust in Him?
2. In what ways have you experienced the stability of God in your own life?
3. Why is it important to recognize Jesus as both the Author and Finisher of our faith?
4. Have you ever been tempted to seek spiritual knowledge outside of God? What led you back to Him?
5. How can you apply the truth that God knows the end from the beginning in your daily decisions and challenges?

- **Cultivate a Deeper Trust**: Intentionally practice trusting God in small daily decisions as well as in significant life choices, reflecting on His eternal nature as a foundation for your trust.
- **Equip Yourself with Scripture**: Regularly study biblical prophecies and promises to deepen your understanding of God's sovereignty and His plans for the future. This will help you to stand firm in your faith during uncertain times.
- **Engage in Faith-Confirming Activities**: Participate in prayer and worship, focusing on God's attributes as the Alpha and Omega. This can reinforce your perception of God's omnipresence and omnipotence in your life.

JOURNALING Prompt

Reflect on a time when you felt uncertain or unstable in your life. How did recognizing God as your Rock and stable foundation change your perspective or situation? Write about how this understanding can guide you in future challenges.

∾

THE ROCK

CHAPTER 18

THE REST

"Entering God's rest allows us to cease our own efforts and rely on His completed works, bringing peace and fulfillment beyond our understanding."

Hebrews 4:10 (NKJV): "For he who has entered His rest has himself also ceased from his works as God did from His."

In this chapter, I want to talk about the amazing benefits of turning to the Rock, or God. These benefits include a special kind of rest that only He can provide. This rest isn't like what we get from sleep or vacations, even though those are great. **The Rock offers a unique rest** that's essential for anyone working with God.

Let's look at a story from the Old Testament that shows this divine rest. When Moses told Joshua to fight the Amalekites, he promised to stand on a hill with the staff of God. As long as Moses held up the staff, the Israelites had the advantage. But when his arms got tired, Aaron and Hur supported them and found a stone for him to sit on. **This stone, or Rock, symbolized**

God supporting Moses, allowing him to rest while achieving great things.

This story shows that we, like Moses, need to become one with God's purpose. When Moses sat on the rock, he wasn't just sitting; he was aligning himself with God's will, turning his actions into divine purpose. **This unity is crucial** for anyone wanting to fulfill God's plans on Earth.

In this spiritual rest, we align seamlessly with God's Word and His purposes. **This state of rest is essential** for those who pray and work in God's service, enabling them to operate from a place of peace and effectiveness.

Think of God's rest as being on a mountaintop, far above the chaos of the natural world, where time constraints don't exist. This timeless perspective was something the prophets experienced, allowing them to see and prophesy events across different periods effortlessly. **This timelessness is a hallmark** of spiritual rest.

God's rest is rooted in the completion of His works. The plan of redemption, for example, was set before the world's foundation. **As believers, we can enter this rest,** recognizing that God's plans are already complete and perfect. This understanding shifts our prayer from asking God to act to discovering His already established will. This discovery is a delight, much like uncovering hidden treasures.

The book of Hebrews gives us insights into different types of rest. It talks about the physical Promised Land, spiritual promises, and the rest God experienced after creation. **These rests symbolize God's finished works** and promises.

Entering God's rest requires faith and obedience. **Unbelief and disobedience prevent access** to this rest. God continually invites us to enter, but we must stop our efforts and embrace His completed works. Encouraging each other in this journey is vital.

REFLECTIVE QUESTIONS

1. How can you shift your understanding of rest from a physical to a spiritual perspective?
2. In what areas of your life do you need to rely more on God's support rather than your own efforts?
3. How can you become more aligned with God's will and purpose?
4. What experiences have you had that mirror the mountaintop and valley analogy of spiritual rest?
5. How can you cultivate a sense of discovery and curiosity in your spiritual journey?

ACTIONABLE STEPS

- **Develop a routine of spiritual rest**: Dedicate time daily for prayer, meditation, and reading Scripture to connect with God and find rest in His presence.
- **Equip yourself with knowledge of God's promises**: Study the Bible to understand the different types of rest God offers and how they apply to your life.
- **Engage in a faith community**: Join a group of believers who encourage each other to enter God's rest, share insights, and support one another in spiritual growth.

JOURNALING Prompt

"Reflect on a time when you felt supported and at rest in God. How did this experience impact your faith and your ability to handle challenges? What steps can you take to cultivate this sense of rest in your daily life?"

$\sim$

THE REST

CHAPTER 19

THE LABOR

"Trust in God's Plan." Remember that God's works are already established, and His plans for you are good. Rest in His presence and let your faith be strengthened by the assurance that He is in control.

"Be still, and know that I am God; I will be exalted among the nations, I will be exalted in the earth!" Psalm 46:10 NKJV

I n this chapter, I want to talk about what it means to labor to enter God's rest. This might sound strange at first—how can rest require labor? But it's an important part of our spiritual journey.

First, let's look at Jesus. He faced the cross with a remarkable sense of peace and rest. King David described it perfectly in Acts 2:25-28 when he spoke of Jesus saying, "I see that the Lord is always with me. I will not be shaken, for he is right beside me. No wonder my heart is glad, and my tongue shouts his praises! My body rests in hope. For you will not leave my soul among the dead or allow your Holy One to rot in the grave. You have shown me the way of life, and you will fill me with the joy of your presence."

As Jesus approached His sacrifice, He wasn't falling apart. He knew His Father's presence was with Him. **Jesus' Confidence** was unshaken, and He could say, "Into Your hands do I commit My spirit." He knew that God wouldn't leave Him dead and that His body wouldn't rot in the grave. Jesus knew the end of the story because He had spent time in God's presence, understanding His Father's plans.

When Jesus invited people to come to Him, He promised them rest. He said, "Come to Me, all you who labor and are heavy laden, and I will give you rest." This **Invitation to Rest** is more than just physical rest—it's a deep, soul-refreshing rest that comes from being in His presence.

There's nothing like the refreshing that His presence gives our souls. It's different from the tiredness we feel when we try to handle everything on our own. When we're worn out from our efforts, Jesus invites us to come to Him. He shows us His will, often through promises or prophecies, which allows us to see the ending according to His plan. This brings **Practical Rest**, where we stop relying on our efforts and trust in God's will.

Hebrews 4:11 tells us to labor to enter this rest. It means doing whatever is necessary to get to that place of spiritual peace. This **Labor to Enter Rest** is not about striving in our strength but about moving into the spirit, where God's will is already established. In that place of rest, we discover what God has already determined, and our prayers are filled with faith because **Rest in Faith** activates everything in God.

Sometimes, our initial prayers may still be filled with natural concerns, and we might feel exhausted. But as we transition to being spiritually aware, we start to rest in God's presence. This **Transitioning to Spiritual Awareness** helps us understand His will and leads to effective, faith-filled prayers.

It's important to recognize that **God's Established Plans** are already in place. When we rest in His presence and understand His plans, we can pray with confidence, knowing that His purposes will prevail. This doesn't mean that things will always be easy, but we can trust that God's works are already done.

Empowerment by the Holy Spirit is crucial in achieving God's purposes. It's not by our power or might but by the Holy Spirit. This spiritual empowerment allows us to accomplish God's works, relying on divine strength rather than our own efforts.

When we believe and have faith, we enter God's rest. **Rest in Faith** means trusting that God's plans are in place, giving us peace and assurance. We stop our frantic efforts and let God work through us.

Prayer as Spiritual Labor happens after we enter rest. It's like the labor of childbirth, bringing God's promises to manifestation. This kind of labor is empowered by faith and aligned with God's established will. For example, Jesus' first coming didn't just happen; it was prayed for by people like Anna, Simeon, Zacharias, and Elizabeth. They were like spiritual midwives, praying until the Messiah came.

The greatest thing Jesus did was not His miracles but His resurrection and our rising with Him. This massive miracle wasn't because of Jesus' exertion but because of His rest in God's promises. True faith is marked by rest, and **Our Greatest Exploits** come from a place of faith and rest.

Let's reflect on some key points and actionable steps to help us understand and apply these concepts in our lives.

REFLECTIVE QUESTIONS

1. How can you shift your focus from natural concerns to spiritual awareness in your daily life?
2. In what ways do you see Jesus' rest and assurance influencing your approach to difficult situations?
3. What practical steps can you take to enter God's rest more consistently in your prayer life?
4. How does understanding that God's works are already established change your perspective on prayer and faith?
5. Reflect on a time when you felt the empowerment of the Holy Spirit. How did it impact your actions and outcomes?

ACTIONABLE STEPS

- **Cultivate:** Develop a routine of spending quiet time with God daily to shift your focus from natural worries to spiritual rest. This practice will help you become more aware of God's presence and plans.
- **Equip:** Equip yourself with scripture and promises that affirm God's established plans. Memorize and meditate on these verses to strengthen your faith and trust in His will.
- **Engage:** Engage in prayer from a place of rest, asking the Holy Spirit to reveal God's will and purposes. Let your prayers be guided by faith and assurance in God's established works.

Journaling **Prompt**

Reflect on a time when you faced a significant challenge. How did your faith and understanding of God's promises help you navigate through that situation? Write about the feelings and insights you experienced as you trusted in God's established plans.

~

THE LABOR

THE SPIRIT REALM OFFICIAL WORKBOOK

CHAPTER 20

DRINKING FROM THE RIVER

"Trust in God's provision." Remember that God's works are already established, and He provides all we need. Rest in His presence and let your faith be strengthened by the assurance that He is in control.

"And my God shall supply all your need according to His riches in glory by Christ Jesus." Philippians 4:19 NKJV

There are two great stories in Exodus 17 that show us how to work with Jesus in prayer. Both stories use a rock to teach us important lessons about God.

First, let's talk about praying from a place of rest, which means resting on the **Rock of Ages**. This is crucial for our prayer life.

In the second story from Exodus 17, the Israelites had no water during their journey in the wilderness. When they complained, Moses prayed, and God told him to strike the rock with his rod. Moses did as he was told, and water gushed out. This is a beautiful picture of Christ as the Rock that was struck.

When Jesus was struck for our sins, life came gushing out instead of anger and vengeance. This miracle of water from the rock saved the lives of the Israelites and gives us a **Miracle of Water from the Rock**.

The **Rock in Exodus** that provided water was actually a representation of Christ. Even though the Israelites didn't realize it, they were drinking from Christ. Jesus hadn't come in the flesh yet, but this event was a preview of how we would interact with Him after He fulfilled God's plan of redemption.

During His ministry, Jesus invited anyone who was thirsty to come to Him and drink. He promised that **Rivers of Living Water** would flow from those who believe in Him, referring to the Holy Spirit. Since Jesus has now entered His glory, the Spirit is given to everyone who believes in Him. This invitation from Jesus is extended to us.

For believers who have been baptized in the Holy Spirit, praying in tongues is a designated way to drink this living water. When you pray in tongues, you are **Drinking Living Water** from Jesus. He identified this water as the Holy Spirit, who I like to think of as "liquid God."

Remember, God is the first and the last, the beginning and the end. This applies to the Holy Spirit too. So when you come to Jesus and drink, you are drinking from a work of God that has already been planned. Often when I pray in tongues, I'm aware that I'm praying about God's purpose that's already been planned and finished but hasn't manifested yet. I'm not praying so God will do something; I'm praying to drink in His purpose and plans. This is **Praying God's Purposes**.

The way you drink water is through your mouth. Similarly, you drink this divine water through your mouth by praying in tongues. When you pray with the purpose of drinking in God's purposes, you're asking, "What are You wanting me to pray about?" In faith, open your mouth to God's perfect work, what

He has already established in heaven, and drink of it. What we haven't seen or heard in this earthly realm doesn't mean it doesn't exist. It's just not manifested yet, but it does exist in God. He invites us to drink in His higher thoughts and ways. **Mouth as the Source** is important here.

God has many glorious victories already commanded. We can facilitate and conduct God's works that are established in heaven through faith-filled prayer, prayer in the Holy Spirit, and inspired prophetic utterance. When we speak what He tells us to, we create a path for His works to be accomplished on earth as they are in heaven. **Facilitating God's Works** is how we bring His plans to life here.

The water from Jesus purifies us, cleansing away distractions and discouragements. It refreshes our spirits and focuses us on God's higher thoughts and ways. When life leaves you feeling thirsty and dry, Jesus invites you to come and drink from Him. Let the Holy Spirit, the living water, do its work in you. This **Purification and Refreshing** is vital.

You drink from one Source: Jesus. Not only is there an endless supply in Him, but for those who drink abundantly, multiple rivers of living water flow through them to others. **Spirit-fed Prayer** is energizing and effective, reaching beyond our own needs.

If it feels like your spiritual spring has dried up, don't try harder. Drink more. Just like a riverbed facilitates water flow, our lives facilitate God's life and plans. If you feel like not much is happening, don't strive more—drink more. The more you drink in, the more divine life flows out. It's effortless. **Effortlessly** let God's life flow through you.

REFLECTIVE QUESTIONS

1. How can you recognize and engage with the spiritual significance of Christ as the Rock in your prayer life?
2. In what ways can you accept Jesus' invitation to drink from Him and experience the living water He offers?
3. How does understanding the Holy Spirit as "liquid God" impact your perspective on praying in tongues?
4. What practical steps can you take to facilitate God's established works in your daily life?
5. Reflect on a time when you felt spiritually refreshed by the Holy Spirit. How did it change your approach to prayer and challenges?

ACTIONABLE STEPS

1. **Cultivate:** Make a habit of daily prayer, focusing on resting in God's presence and aligning your thoughts with His higher plans and purposes.
2. **Equip:** Learn and meditate on scriptures that emphasize the life-giving power of Jesus as the Rock and the Holy Spirit as living water. Let these scriptures guide your prayers.
3. **Engage:** Actively pray in tongues, asking the Holy Spirit to reveal God's purposes. Trust that you are drinking in His divine will and plans, refreshing your soul and empowering your actions.

Journaling Prompt

Reflect on a time when you experienced spiritual dryness. How did you seek and find refreshment in God's presence? Write about how drinking from Jesus, the living water, transformed your situation and perspective.

∽

CHAPTER 21

THE PURPOSES OF GOD

"Embrace Your Purpose." Remember that God has a specific purpose and plan for your life. Trust in His guidance and seek His will, knowing that He has predestined you for good works.

"For I know the thoughts that I think toward you, says the Lord, thoughts of peace and not of evil, to give you a future and a hope." Jeremiah 29:11 NKJV

Some people live from moment to moment without a plan. While spontaneity can be fun, living a whole life with no plan or purpose is chaotic. God is the opposite of this. **God's Intentional Planning** means He has clear purposes and plans for everything He does. None of His actions are random; they are all intentionally based on His purposes and contribute to His overall plan.

Jesus didn't just show up and wing it when He came to earth. **Jesus' Pre-ordained Purpose** was established before He was born. His mission to redeem us was planned long ago. The details of His life were written in God's book, like a script. Jesus was born on purpose, for a purpose.

Throughout His life, Jesus was aware of His Father's purpose and dedicated Himself to fulfilling it. He said His nourishment came from doing God's will and completing His work. **Jesus' Commitment to God's Will** shows us that He chose to follow God's plan, especially in the garden of Gethsemane before His passion.

Mary, Jesus' mother, was also born for a divine purpose. When Gabriel told her about God's plan for her, she accepted it willingly. **Mary's Acceptance of God's Plan** made her a unique conduit for the redemptive plan. She said, "I am the servant of the Lord. Let it happen to me as you have said."

Jesus' followers had specific tasks assigned by the Father too. **Jesus' Followers and Their Purpose** shows that just like Jesus and Mary, His disciples had definite purposes to fulfill. Jesus told them to carry out the tasks assigned to them because the time to work was limited.

Like Jesus and His disciples, our purpose existed before we were born. **Our Predestined Purpose** is planned by God, and He created good works for us to do. These works and details are written in God's plan and His Word. Our lives are connected to God's definite purposes.

God's love for us is unwavering and doesn't change whether we follow His plans or not. **God's Unwavering Love** means that even if we fail, His love never ends. But there is a special pleasure in bringing delight to God by living according to His purpose. If we love Him, we will want to bring Him joy.

What pleases God is carrying out His purpose. **Pleasing God by Fulfilling His Purpose** was shown when God twice said He was pleased with Jesus—once at His baptism and again at the Transfiguration. This pleasure came from Jesus' obedience and fulfillment of God's will.

Discovering God's Purposes is crucial for us. All of God's purposes are established in Him and can be accessed through His Word and presence. By seeking Him, we can discover our individual purpose and other parts of His plan. This discovery is more valuable than finding a vault of diamonds.

The Holy Spirit pleads for us in our prayers, in harmony with God's will. **The Holy Spirit's Role** is to help us pray according to God's purposes. As a result, God works all these details together for His plan and our good, demonstrating His intelligence and care.

There are some people who live from moment to moment. They don't think about what they are going to do next until right before they do it. While a spontaneous moment can be fun, living an entire life with no plan or purpose is not fun. It's crazy!

God is different from this. **God has purposes, and He has plans** that help fulfill those purposes. None of His words or actions are random. They are intentionally based on His purpose and contribute beautifully to His other purposes. Because of this, when Jesus came to earth, He didn't just show up and "wing it."

According to 1 Peter 1:20, Jesus' purpose of redeeming us existed before He was born. **The details of that purpose** and what Jesus was to do during His time on earth were already planned and written in God's book, similar to a script for a character in a play. Jesus was actually born on purpose, for a purpose.

Jesus was aware of His Father's purpose and dedicated Himself to fulfilling it. He said His nourishment came from doing God's will and completing His work. **Jesus' commitment to God's will** is evident in His teachings and miracles, which the Father gave Him to accomplish. He brought glory to God on earth by completing the work given to Him.

Jesus' purpose wasn't forced on Him. He chose it throughout His life, especially in the garden of Gethsemane before His crucifixion. Mary, Jesus' mother, was also born for God's purpose, yet

God didn't force that purpose on her. **Mary accepted God's plan** willingly, saying, "I am the servant of the Lord. I want it to happen to me just like that."

Jesus' followers also had specific tasks assigned to them by the Father. **Jesus let them know that they had purposes to fulfill** as well. We must carry out the tasks assigned to us by the one who sent us because the time to work is limited.

Not only Jesus and His disciples, but we too are born for a purpose. **Our lives are attached to God's purposes.** Ephesians 2:10 tells us that we are re-created people who will fulfill the destiny given to each of us. Our purpose existed before we were born, and God planned in advance the good works we would do.

Within God's many purposes, each of us has a part. **God's love for us is unwavering** and doesn't change based on what we do. Even if we fail to fulfill His purpose for our lives, His love never ends. However, there is unique pleasure in bringing delight to God by reflecting and expressing His divine purpose in our life.

If we love and cherish God, we want to bring delight to Him. **Living a life that matches God's intention** brings Him pleasure. This is why Paul prayed nonstop for the church in Colossae, asking God to give them complete knowledge of His will and spiritual wisdom and understanding. Then their lives would honor and please the Lord, producing every kind of good fruit and growing as they learned to know God better.

What pleases God is when His purpose is carried out. **Jesus was fully pleasing to the Father** because He fully carried out the will of God and His purpose for Jesus' life. Jesus' purpose as the Redeemer of the world was unique, but He isn't the only one vital to bringing God's purposes from Heaven to earth. We all have been born for His purposes, and it was for those purposes we were born!

Some people live and die never knowing their life had a divine purpose. **Ignorance of God's purpose** doesn't mean they didn't have one. They just didn't know it. When you don't know your purpose, anything can make you wander or turn around. Purpose makes a person and a pray-er resolute.

God's purpose is essential to an individual, group, the Body of Christ, or a nation. **A person, family, group, or nation goes nowhere of eternal value** outside of God's purpose. All of God's purposes are established in Him and can be accessed through His Word and presence. When people go there, details of God's purposes can be discovered by the help and direction of the Holy Spirit. The discovery of these purposes is more valuable than finding a vault of diamonds.

The Holy Spirit pleads for us in our prayer, **in harmony with God's will**. As a result, God works all these details together for His plan and our good. This takes the mind and intelligence of God to accomplish.

REFLECTIVE QUESTIONS

1. How can you recognize and engage with the specific purpose God has for your life?
2. In what ways can you follow Jesus' example of commitment to God's will and purpose?
3. What steps can you take to discover and align with God's purposes for you?
4. How does understanding that God's love is unwavering impact your approach to fulfilling His purposes?
5. Reflect on a time when you felt guided by the Holy Spirit. How did it influence your actions and decisions?

ACTIONABLE STEPS

- **Cultivate:** Make a habit of daily prayer and meditation, asking God to reveal His specific purposes for your life. Spend time in His Word to understand His plans.
- **Equip:** Memorize and meditate on scriptures that emphasize God's intentional planning and purposes. Let these scriptures guide your daily actions and decisions.
- **Engage:** Actively seek the guidance of the Holy Spirit in your prayers, trusting that He will lead you in harmony with God's will. Be open to the tasks and assignments God has planned for you.

JOURNALING **Prompt**

Reflect on a time when you experienced spiritual dryness. How did you seek and find refreshment in God's presence? Write about how drinking from Jesus, the living water, transformed your situation and perspective.

∽

CHAPTER 22

GEARS

"God's plans are revealed in His presence." Spend time with God, trusting that He will reveal His purposes and guide you in every step. His plans are for your good, bringing clarity and direction to your life.

"Call to Me, and I will answer you, and show you great and mighty things, which you do not know." Jeremiah 33:3 NKJV

"There will be a collaboration of operations." This phrase came to me from the Lord in early 2020. I knew it was true for the purposes in both kingdoms of light and darkness. I saw that previously isolated and disconnected purposes would now move together, affecting and activating each other.

To help us understand spiritual concepts, the Lord often uses natural examples. Gears were His way of explaining how these plans and purposes work together. Gears come in different sizes and can move in opposite directions. The teeth of one gear fit between the teeth of another gear. This way, the movement of one gear brings motion to the others they engage with, causing them all to move together.

If a gear didn't have teeth, it would just be a rotating cylinder. Similarly, if it isn't close enough to another gear for their teeth to engage, there wouldn't be any productive function. **Each spiritual purpose is like a gear.** And like gears, each purpose or operation in either kingdom has teeth. The teeth of a kingdom purpose are the plans and details required to bring the purpose to pass.

Details and plans for God's purposes are as important as teeth are to gears. They help move the purpose along. Also, like the teeth of a gear, there isn't just one detail in God's purposes; there are many! Those in prophetic prayer ministry for God's purposes often pray about these details or plans by which the purposes come to pass.

When the Captain of the Lord of Hosts talked with Joshua before the Israelites advanced on Jericho, He drew Joshua's attention to how things would end because, in God, the victory of Jericho was already established. "See! I have given Jericho into your hand, its king, and the mighty men of valor," the Lord said to Joshua (Joshua 6:2 NKJV). What a glorious prophecy! It was true and powerful. However, Joshua didn't immediately rally the troops and storm Jericho. There were **details and plans, important and meticulous ones, yet to be revealed.** These plans had sequence and order and took place over several days. The details allowed Joshua and the army of Israel to respond to God in the obedience of faith.

Joshua didn't make these details up. Caleb didn't present Joshua with a plan drawn from his thoughts. **These practical ways to participate in God's plan came from God!** That's what gives us the advantage over the enemy. These plans cannot be discovered except in the presence of God.

"No eye has seen, no ear has heard, and no mind has imagined what God has prepared for those who love him. But it was to us that God revealed these things by His Spirit. For His Spirit searches out everything and shows us God's deep secrets. No one can know a person's thoughts except that person's own spirit, and no one can know God's thoughts except God's own Spirit. And we have received God's Spirit (not the world's spirit), so we can know the wonderful things God has freely given us" (1 Corinthians 2:9-12 NLT).

Notice that the Holy Spirit shows us the details already in God. Until these details are revealed and understood, they are a mystery. That's why **praying in tongues is such a benefit**. In this way, we can actually have discussions and conversations with God about the details of His purpose before our minds know what they are. Tongues are a part of the process by which we can begin to understand these details in God.

"For he who speaks in a tongue does not speak to men but to God, for no one understands him; however, in the spirit, he speaks mysteries" (1 Corinthians 14:2 NKJV). "So too the [Holy] Spirit comes to our aid and bears us up in our weakness; for we do not know what prayer to offer nor how to offer it worthily as we ought, but the Spirit Himself goes to meet our supplication and pleads in our behalf with unspeakable yearnings and groanings too deep for utterance" (Romans 8:26 AMPC). "God, the searcher of the heart, knows fully our longings, yet He also understands the desires of the Spirit, because the Holy Spirit passionately pleads before God for us, His holy ones, in perfect harmony with God's plan and our destiny. So we are convinced that every detail of our lives is continually woven together to fit into God's perfect plan of bringing good into our lives, for we are His lovers who have been called to fulfill His designed purpose" (Romans 8:27-28 TPT).

The advantages of praying in other tongues are beyond our comprehension, especially when there is an interpretation of these prayers. One of the gifts of the Spirit is the interpretation of tongues, which follows another gift of the Spirit, which is tongues. These two gifts provide a powerful ministry. I've experienced and witnessed these gifts working together to unfold doctrine, inject truth and direction, and reveal aspects of God's will.

These particular gifts of the Spirit are within a list of all nine of the Spirit's gifts (1 Corinthians 12:8-11). Tongues and interpretation of tongues as gifts of the Spirit are given as the Spirit wills and determines, and through whom He chooses. These are different from the tongues and interpretation spoken of in 1 Corinthians 14, which is activated as the believer wills to do the instruction he is given. Paul also gave instruction regarding interpretation: "So anyone who speaks in tongues should pray also for the ability to interpret what has been said" (1 Corinthians 14:13 NLT).

Here we have clear instructions to not just pray in tongues but to take the next step and ask for the interpretation of what we have been praying. **Interpretations of tongues can come in a variety of ways.** Here are some that I have experienced.

Interpretations that immediately follow prayer in tongues can be similar to translating phrases. It's not a word-by-word translation but more of a general paraphrase of the message. During the prayer in other tongues, there could also come a name, place, word, or a phrase or sentence in your own language or understanding. These come like singular pieces of a puzzle. By themselves, they don't mean much, but together with other pieces of God's will, they can begin to display a picture. It's important not to disregard these pieces, and it is equally important not to make them mean something they don't. Again, treat them like puzzle pieces.

Dreams after the time of prayer in tongues also bring a form of interpretation. Someone else, unknowingly, may give an inspired teaching or prophecy that brings to light and understanding what was prayed before. Another type of interpretation could come after the time of prayer to bring thoughts and awareness to God's thoughts and ways.

I encourage you to use your faith, not only in praying mysteries in other tongues but also in interpreting your prayers. **Interpretations can come immediately or later**, but expect them to come. After those mysteries become clearly defined details in God's plan, we can see how there is no way to do God's plans without His revealed ways (Isaiah 55:8-9).

Let's give ourselves time in His presence where His secret plans are kept. He doesn't keep them from us. He keeps them for us.

"Position yourself before My face. Receive My mercy and my grace. My purpose for you I will show. The next step to take, you will certainly know."

Let's look at what the Lord told Jeremiah when he was imprisoned in the court of the guard—a confined and difficult place in the natural realm. "Thus says the Lord Who made [the earth], the Lord Who formed it to establish it—the Lord is His name: Call to Me, and I will answer you and show you great and mighty things, fenced in and hidden, which you do not know (do not distinguish and recognize, have knowledge of and understand)" (Jeremiah 33:2-3 AMPC).

Jeremiah was unconfined when he got in the spirit. The rest of Jeremiah 33 is full of prophecy regarding his time and hope for the future. It even includes and unfolds into a Messianic prophecy. What a glorious chapter for someone whose physical location in the first verse begins in a prison. From Jeremiah's place in the prison, he was able to call on the Lord and get in the spirit where amazing details in God's plan were revealed that gave him a wide perspective and contributed to the coming Messiah.

. . .

REFLECTIVE QUESTIONS

1. How can you see the collaboration of operations in your spiritual life and in the world around you?
2. In what ways can you use the concept of gears to understand the interaction of different spiritual purposes?
3. What steps can you take to be more aware of the details and plans God has for His purposes in your life?
4. How can praying in tongues and seeking interpretation enhance your understanding of God's will?
5. Reflect on a time when you received a revelation or insight during a challenging situation. How did it change your perspective and actions?

ACTIONABLE STEPS

- **Cultivate:** Develop a regular practice of praying in tongues, asking the Holy Spirit to reveal God's detailed plans and purposes for your life.
- **Equip:** Study and meditate on scriptures that highlight the importance of God's plans and the role of the Holy Spirit in revealing them. Use these scriptures as a foundation for your prayers.
- **Engage:** Actively seek interpretations of your prayers in tongues. Be open to receiving insights through

dreams, inspired teachings, or prophetic words, and apply these revelations to your daily life.

JOURNALING Prompt

Reflect on a time when you experienced spiritual dryness. How did you seek and find refreshment in God's presence? Write about how drinking from Jesus, the living water, transformed your situation and perspective.

∼

CHAPTER 23
DELIGHT IN THE DETAILS

God's plans are intricate and detailed, and He delights in revealing them to those who seek Him earnestly in prayer. Trust that your prayers, no matter how small or insignificant they seem, play a vital role in His grand design.

"For I know the thoughts that I think toward you, says the Lord, thoughts of peace and not of evil, to give you a future and a hope." - Jeremiah 29:11 (NKJV)

When I pray in tongues, I often see five categories of divine details that help us understand God's plans better: **What, Who, Where, When, and Wealth**. These categories, which all start with either W or P, were part of an interpretation during a prayer session. Understanding these categories can bring clarity and light when working with God on the details they represent.

The purpose behind God sending Jesus is clearly stated in John 3:14-17. **Jesus was sent to be the Savior of the world**. The scripture says, "Just as Moses lifted up the snake in the wilderness, so the Son of Man must be lifted up, that everyone who believes may have eternal life in him. For God so loved the world that he gave his one and only Son, that whoever believes in him shall not perish but have eternal life. For God did not send his Son into the world to condemn the world, but to save the world through him." Knowing this divine purpose strengthens our faith and focus in prayer.

Just like the first coming of Jesus, all of God's purposes are carried out by people. Your time in prayer might be for an individual or groups of people. They could be as significant as Mary and Joseph were in Jesus' first coming. Mary's role in the purpose of Redemption was incredibly significant, and Joseph, chosen to be Jesus' stepfather, was not a random choice. He was born for that purpose.

Others in the "Christmas story," like the shepherds, wise men, political leaders, Zacharias and Elizabeth, John the Baptist, and the angelic choir, also had significant roles. Some people involved aren't even mentioned in scripture. Sometimes, **God reveals the names of people who are part of His purpose through prayer**, whether we know them or not. These people, who we pray for, may seem important or simple, like the shepherds, but everyone in God's purposes carries out something vital and necessary.

You may or may not know the people you're led to pray for. They could be believers or non-believers. Be confident that you're praying for the destinies of individuals in God's purposes. He will guide you to pray so people can be empowered to do what they're meant to do.

For example, about four years before the 9/11 terrorist attacks, a prayer group I was part of had a member praying for a person named Osama Bin Laden. None of us had heard this name before, but she felt led by God to pray for him daily. While the 9/11 event wasn't averted, its effects were lessened, and this person's prayers played a part in that. Similarly, Isaiah 45:1 mentions King Cyrus long before he was born, showing that **God knows His purposes and the people involved in them well in advance.**

When praying for people by name, it's interesting to think about whether everyone with that name gets prayed for. Though we don't know for sure, it's not unlike God to maximize the impact of our prayers.

Not only does God lead us to pray for specific people, but also for places important to His plan. You might wonder why a certain city or country keeps coming to mind. It's not just because you live there or want to visit. God has a design and plan that includes that place, and there are often prophecies about it.

For instance, **Jesus had to be born in Bethlehem.** Micah 5:2 says, "But you, O Bethlehem Ephrathah, are only a small village among all the people of Judah. Yet a ruler of Israel, whose origins are in the distant past, will come from you on my behalf." Jesus' exit from the earth also had to be from Jerusalem, as He prophesied in Matthew 16:21: "From then on Jesus began to tell his disciples plainly that it was necessary for him to go to Jerusalem, and that he would suffer many terrible things at the hands of the elders, the leading priests, and the teachers of religious law. He would be killed, but on the third day he would be raised from the dead."

Many people are led to pray for a specific nation, state, region, city, or suburb. These prayers can cover anything from a move of God to political matters. Even if we don't understand why a place is significant to God, we should follow the Spirit's lead and pray, making prayer an adventure.

God's purposes are fulfilled in **His perfect timing.** Jesus was born at the perfect time. 1 Peter 1:20 says, "Before the world began, God had already chosen Christ. But now, during these last days of the world, God has shown Christ to people.

God did that so that he could help you." Galatians 4:4 adds, "But when the right time finally came, God sent his own Son. He came as the son of a human mother and lived under the Jewish Law."

Prayer often accompanies God's purposes over time, with intensity increasing as the fulfillment nears. Like labor pains before a birth, the urge to pray intensifies. Once-a-week prayer meetings might turn into more frequent and longer sessions, with yearning and groaning for God's will (Romans 8:22-27).

Anna is a great example. As the time for Jesus' birth grew near, she prayed day and night in the temple. Simeon also dedicated himself to seeing God's will come to pass. They were perfectly aligned to witness the manifestation of their prayers when Jesus was presented to the Lord.

In prayer ministry, **we labor to enter "the rest" where God's purposes are preordained** (Hebrews 4:11). From that place of rest, we work with the Spirit to bring those purposes into reality. Prayers can give birth to destinies that already exist in God. This time will see divine ministries and magnificent, unheard-of things born, much like Jesus in the fullness of time. Some ministries are not yet birthed, and current-day spiritual midwives help these purposes come to pass, just as Anna, Simeon, Zacharias, and Elizabeth did with Jesus.

God provides for His purposes. The wise men's gifts were perfectly timed for Jesus' family's emergency trip to Egypt, showing that God funds His own plans. Wealth can be laid up in unexpected places, and it's not just for meeting our needs. While divine provision for our needs is promised to those who seek first the kingdom, we can also expect provision for the purposes we are to carry out.

The journey to fulfilling God's purposes is an adventure full of divine details. Each detail holds great value, and delighting in them makes the journey worthwhile.

. . .

REFLECTIVE QUESTIONS

1. What specific divine purpose has God revealed to you in your life?
2. Who are the people you feel led to pray for regularly, and how might they be part of God's purpose?
3. Are there specific places that hold significant spiritual importance to you?
4. How do you discern God's perfect timing in your life?
5. In what ways have you experienced God's provision for His purposes in your life?

ACTIONABLE STEPS

- **Cultivate a Habit of Praying for Divine Details**: Set aside dedicated time daily to pray specifically for the categories of What, Who, Where, When, and Wealth. Keep a prayer journal to record any revelations or impressions.
- **Equip Yourself with Knowledge of God's Word**: Study scriptures related to God's purposes and promises. Familiarize yourself with stories of divine purpose, people, places, timing, and provision.
- **Engage in Intense and Persistent Prayer**: Join or form a prayer group focused on interceding for God's purposes. Encourage each other to stay persistent and increase the intensity of your prayers as you sense God's timing approaching.

. . .

Journaling Prompt

Reflect on a time when you sensed a clear divine purpose or direction in your life. Write about the people, places, timing, and provision involved in that experience. How did this revelation impact your faith and prayers?

∽

CHAPTER 24
PREPARING THE WAY OF THE LORD

As we continue on our paths, both literal and spiritual, let's embrace the journey with patience and joy. Each step, guided by the Holy Spirit, is part of a much larger story of love and redemption that God is unfolding. Remember, as we keep doing good and remain steadfast in our efforts, we are promised that in due season we will reap the benefits if we do not lose heart.

"Let us not grow weary while doing good, for in due season we shall reap if we do not lose heart." - Galatians 6:9 (NKJV)

In Chapter 24 of our journey together, titled "Preparing the Way of the Lord," I share an analogy between the constant construction on a highway my friend Tony and I frequently use and our own spiritual journeys. This chapter opens with our routine drive to church, taking a route that, although quickest, is often under construction. This scenario, though it might seem just a part of everyday life, offers a deeper lesson about the **ongoing nature of both road construction and our spiritual development.**

Much like the continuous construction on that highway, our **spiritual growth and prayer efforts aren't quick tasks**; they require sustained effort and commitment. This teaches us that true development, whether in infrastructure or in our spiritual lives, takes time, dedication, and persistence.

Tony enjoys this route because he gets to see the **progress being made on the highway**. Similarly, in our spiritual walks, noticing even small improvements can be hugely encouraging. Acknowledging these milestones reminds us that each step forward, no matter how small, is significant and contributes to our ultimate goals.

Just as physical barricades are used to guide and protect traffic through construction zones, we encounter **spiritual "barricades" that redirect and shape our spiritual path**. These challenges can be disruptive, but they are essential for our growth, helping us to remain flexible and responsive to God's guidance.

There's a common misunderstanding that prayer is something we can do quickly, expecting immediate results. However, effective prayer, much like road construction, is an **ongoing process**. It requires continuous effort and doesn't always show immediate effects, but it is crucial for long-term spiritual health and fulfillment of God's plans.

The scripture from Isaiah 40:3-5 lays out a vision of making a **straight path for the Lord**, which includes filling valleys and smoothing rough spots. This passage serves as a blueprint for how we should prepare ourselves spiritually—by making our lives and hearts ready for God's work.

The Holy Spirit plays a crucial role in our spiritual lives, similar to an operations manager in a construction project. He guides us, gives us strength, and ensures that each task we undertake is in alignment with God's larger plan, helping us to work efficiently and purposefully.

Just like a complex construction project requires a team with diverse skills, the **spiritual work within the Church involves various members** each contributing in unique but important ways. This collaboration ensures that God's overarching plan is accomplished effectively and beautifully.

Reflecting on John the Baptist's role as the one who prepared the way for Jesus connects us to a long history of individuals called to pave the way for spiritual renewal. This continuity shows that our current spiritual efforts are linked to a broader, divine narrative that spans centuries.

Picture our collective prayer efforts as **supporting pillars holding up a grand structure**. Each pillar has a specific role and, while serving its individual purpose, supports a larger, grander vision. This metaphor helps us see the interconnectedness and importance of each prayer and action within the Church.

As we approach what many believe to be the end times, our separate spiritual efforts are beginning to **converge and align more closely**. This growing together is not only exciting but also a powerful reminder of the significance of our work in God's grand scheme.

REFLECTIVE QUESTIONS

1. How does recognizing small milestones in your life encourage you in your spiritual walk?
2. When have you encountered spiritual "barricades" that altered your path, and how did you respond?
3. In what ways can you prepare yourself for the long-term nature of spiritual and prayerful commitments?
4. How can you better recognize and cooperate with the

Holy Spirit's guidance in your everyday decisions and tasks?

5. What are ways you can more actively engage with and contribute to the collective efforts of your spiritual community?

ACTIONABLE STEPS

- **Cultivate Patience and Persistence in Spiritual Practices** - Develop habits that foster long-term commitment and patience, such as regular reflection on scriptural promises and the progress you've made, understanding that spiritual growth is a gradual process.
- **Equip Yourself with Biblical and Prophetic Understanding** - Study biblical prophecies and teachings that relate to spiritual preparation and the roles of different figures in the Bible, to better understand your part in God's plans.
- **Engage Actively in Community Prayer Efforts** - Participate in or initiate prayer groups that focus on communal and global issues, enhancing the collective prayer effort and your personal contribution to God's work.

JOURNALING Prompt

Reflect on the current 'construction projects' in your spiritual life. What are the 'highways' you are building towards God?

Consider the tools (spiritual disciplines, community support, etc.) that you are using and the obstacles you are overcoming. Write down how these efforts are preparing the way for deeper faith and greater works in God's plan.

~

THE SPIRIT REALM OFFICIAL WORKBOOK

155

CHAPTER 25
THE JEWS, THE NATIONS, AND THE CHURCH

As we serve in our various capacities, let's remember that each of us is crucial to the body of Christ. Your unique contributions help build up the Church and advance God's kingdom on Earth. Embrace your role, knowing that in the diversity of our tasks, there is a beautiful unity that reflects God's wisdom and love.

"But you are a chosen generation, a royal priesthood, a holy nation, His own special people, that you may proclaim the praises of Him who called you out of darkness into His marvelous light." - 1 Peter 2:9 (NKJV)

I n Chapter 25, titled "The Jews, the Nations, and the Church," I use the intricate design of the human body to illustrate how every one of us in the body of Christ plays a unique and crucial role. Like each organ in our bodies that has a specific function, every member of the Church is tasked with specific spiritual roles. This chapter unpacks the beauty of our individual contributions and how they tie into the larger purpose of God's kingdom, emphasizing the need for both diversity and unity within the Church.

Just as our bodies are complex and each part serves a specific purpose, so is the **body of Christ** designed. Each of us has a **distinct role** that contributes to the whole, much like how our physical organs work in harmony to keep us healthy and active. It's amazing to see how God has mirrored this intricate design in both our physical and spiritual lives.

Just as the lungs have a different function from the heart, each of us is given specific tasks in the spiritual realm. Realizing our **unique roles** helps us to focus on what we are meant to do, rather than getting caught up in what others are doing. This helps us to fully engage in our own spiritual duties without distraction.

The way each part of our body relies on the others to function properly illustrates how we, as members of the Church, need to work together. If one part suffers, the whole body feels it. Similarly, the Church thrives when each of us is actively and effectively **fulfilling our roles**, showing how critical unity is to our collective strength and mission.

Paul categorizes humanity into three key groups—Jews, Gentiles, and the Church—to help us understand different spiritual responsibilities. This classification not only guides our prayers but also shapes our understanding of the **global mission** we are part of, ensuring that our prayers and actions are well-directed.

When people join the Church, they become part of a spiritual nation, a transformation that transcends previous national or ethnic identities. This new identity, as God's chosen people, is deeper than any earthly bond and calls us to **live out a divine purpose**.

The Church is described not just as a gathering but as an **eternal kingdom**, emphasizing the lasting impact of our spiritual lives. This perspective encourages us to see our roles within the Church not just as temporary tasks but as contributions to a lasting spiritual legacy.

Our diverse prayer assignments—for Jews, nations, or the Church at large—are part of God's strategic plan for spreading His love and salvation across the earth. Recognizing our **specific assignments** helps us engage more meaningfully in God's broader mission.

The Holy Spirit's guidance is crucial in ensuring our prayers are not only heartfelt but also effective and targeted. His promptings help us to focus our prayers where they are most needed, aligning our intentions with **God's plans**.

The call to pray for more laborers in the harvest fields is a universal mandate from Jesus that applies to every believer. This highlights the ongoing need for dedicated individuals to spread the gospel, underlining the importance of **these prayers**.

The variety in our prayer assignments reflects the vast scope of God's plan and showcases the beauty of our shared mission. This diversity should be celebrated, as it enriches our collective experience and enhances our effectiveness in fulfilling **God's work on earth**.

REFLECTIVE QUESTIONS

1. How does understanding your specific role in the body of Christ affect your spiritual activities and choices?
2. What are practical ways you can contribute to the unity and effectiveness of your local church community?
3. How has your identity as a member of the Church

    influenced your interactions with people from
different backgrounds?

4. Are there particular groups or issues that you feel
called to pray for more fervently? Why do you think
this is?

5. How can you better support or engage with different
ministries within your church or community, even if
they are not your primary areas of calling?

ACTIONABLE STEPS

- **Cultivate an Awareness of Your Spiritual Role** -
Take time to prayerfully consider what specific role
you might have within the body of Christ. Seek
confirmation through scripture, prayer, and counsel
from trusted spiritual leaders.

- **Equip Yourself with Knowledge on Global
Christian Issues** - Educate yourself about the
different challenges and needs facing the Church
globally. This could involve studying scripture,
reading books on global Christianity, or attending
seminars and workshops.

- **Engage in Targeted Prayer** - Actively participate in
prayer groups or initiatives that focus on the Jews,
the nations, or the global Church. Your prayers can
have a powerful impact on these crucial areas of
God's kingdom work.

Journaling Prompt

Reflect on what it means to you to be part of a "holy nation" as described in 1 Peter 2:9. How does this identity influence your view of your role in the Church and your interactions with the world? Consider ways you can more effectively live out this calling to show others the goodness of God.

∼

ʾINDIVIDUALS

Remember, each prompting to pray is an opportunity to participate in God's work. Whether it's a fleeting thought or a deep concern for someone, your prayers can have eternal implications. Embrace these moments with faith, knowing that you are a vital **conduit of God's grace and mercy.**

"Confess your trespasses to one another, and pray for one another, that you may be healed. The effective, fervent prayer of a righteous man avails much." - James 5:16 (NKJV)

In Chapter 26, "Individuals," I explore how we can be moved to pray for specific people, much like Jesus was when he felt compelled to pray for Peter. This sensitivity to others' needs through the Holy Spirit is a central theme of the chapter, illustrating how personal and direct our prayer lives can be.

Spiritual Sensitivity Toward Individuals plays a crucial role in how we connect with and support each other in faith. Just as Jesus sensed Peter's upcoming challenges and prayed for him,

THE SPIRIT REALM OFFICIAL WORKBOOK

we too might feel a pull on our hearts to pray for someone specific—signaling the Holy Spirit's guidance.

Understanding Promptings for Prayer can sometimes appear as subtle hints in our daily thoughts. Perhaps someone's image comes to mind unexpectedly or repeatedly. Recognizing these moments as cues from the Holy Spirit is the first step towards making a meaningful impact through our prayers.

The Role of the Holy Spirit in Highlighting Needs is to guide us towards those who need our prayers the most, often before we even know why. It's important to respond to these promptings with prayer and support rather than judgment or criticism.

It is crucial to **Distinguish Between Holy Spirit and Accusatory Thoughts**. If your thoughts about someone lean towards criticism, it's likely not from the Holy Spirit. The enemy, or accuser, plants these thoughts to sow judgment and division, unlike the Holy Spirit, who prompts us towards compassion and aid.

When Jesus prayed for Peter, He focused on ensuring that Peter's **faith would not fail**, rather than on preventing his denial. This teaches us that our prayers should concentrate on strengthening faith, helping others to find their way back even after they falter.

Impact of Responsive Prayer is profound. By answering God's call to pray, we often gain deeper insights into the person's circumstances, enabling us to pray more effectively. This responsiveness not only changes lives but deepens our connection with God.

Simply **Remembering Someone** might seem trivial, but in the realm of prayer, it can be the start of something divine. Such remembrances, when turned into prayers, act as channels through which God works His will and purposes.

Prayer as a Channel of Supernatural Activity underscores that our responses to these everyday occurrences can unlock powerful spiritual actions. What might seem like a natural recollection can actually be a stepping stone to supernatural interventions.

Engaging in **Continuous Revelation Through Prayer** means that the more actively we respond to prayer promptings, the more God reveals. This cycle of revelation and response enhances our prayer effectiveness and deepens our spiritual journey.

Jesus' Example of Constant Responsiveness serves as a model for us. His life was a testament to the impact of consistently responding to the Father's guidance, whether it was a call to pray, heal, or intervene. His responsiveness resulted in a life that was a vibrant display of God's power and love.

This chapter invites you to reflect on how you respond to the Holy Spirit's subtle signals in your life. Consider how a simple thought of someone might be your cue to engage in prayer that could have significant implications. Embrace these promptings with readiness and see how they expand your experience of God's active presence in the world.

REFLECTIVE QUESTIONS

1. How can you become more attuned to recognizing when the Holy Spirit is prompting you to pray for someone?

2. Are your thoughts about others leading you to pray constructively for them, or do they lean toward judgment?

3. Do your prayers focus more on preventing failure or fostering spiritual growth and resilience?

4. Can you recall a time when remembering someone led you to pray for them? What was the outcome?
5. How has responding to prayer promptings changed your prayer life or the lives of those you have prayed for?

ACTIONABLE STEPS

- **Cultivate a Prayerful Attitude Toward Remembrances** - Train yourself to view each remembrance of an individual as a potential divine prompting to pray. This mindset will help you become a more proactive intercessor.
- **Equip Yourself With Knowledge About Discerning Spirits** - Learn more about discerning the origins of your thoughts—whether they stem from the Holy Spirit, your own mind, or negative sources. This knowledge can help you focus on constructive prayer.
- **Engage in Daily Responsive Prayer** - Set aside time each day to pray responsively. Start with whoever comes to mind and ask God for guidance on how to pray for them, making your prayer life a dynamic dialogue with God.

JOURNALING Prompt

Reflect on the times you've felt prompted to pray for some-one. Write about these experiences, noting any outcomes you observed or insights you received during or after your prayers. Consider how these moments have shaped your understanding of God's work through your prayers.

～

CHAPTER 27

CONTEND FOR THE DESTINIES

In the complexities and challenges of life, your prayers are powerful and effective. They reach beyond the immediate, touching destinies and unfolding God's purposes across time and space. Keep contending in prayer; your intercession is a vital part of God's plan.

"The effective, fervent prayer of a righteous man avails much." (James 5:16b, NKJV)

In Chapter 27, I open up about a moment when I started praying intensely for a newborn in another country, hoping desperately for his recovery. But as I prayed, something unexpected happened: I felt a divine nudge, a message that shifted my focus from one child to a broader battle—the **destinies of many**.

This experience showed me how prayer isn't just about asking for things; it's a connection that can open our eyes to bigger truths and challenges. As I stood in the church, praying, I realized that my prayers were part of a bigger picture. This wasn't just about one baby's life; it was about engaging in a deeper, more widespread fight for the future of many souls.

I remembered the story of King David and his first child with Bathsheba, a story where intense prayer seemed to end in sorrow. Yet, I wondered if David's prayers were actually laying the groundwork for something greater—his next son, Solomon, who would be significant not just to their family but to the whole story of our faith. This reflection helped me see that our prayers, even when they seem unanswered, are **woven into a larger, divine plan**.

The chapter goes deep into the idea that our destinies are often **contested by spiritual forces**. Just like significant figures from the Bible—like Moses, who was targeted by Pharaoh, or Jesus, who was hunted by Herod—our own paths are also challenged by forces that want to steer us away from our divine purpose. Recognizing this battle, our prayers become vital defenses, not just for ourselves but for the destinies of others as well.

Paul the Apostle knew the importance of community in these battles. He often sought the **prayers of the early Christians**, knowing that facing spiritual challenges needed more than one person's effort. His letters asking for prayer support remind us of the power that comes from praying together, supporting each other in our spiritual journeys.

Prophecies, too, play a crucial role in our spiritual life. They aren't just foretelling the future; they **equip us to stand firm against challenges**. By holding on to prophetic words, we are armed with reminders of God's promises, giving us strength and direction in the midst of our struggles.

This chapter also taught me that when we follow God's call, it's about more than the task at hand—we are being **shaped and changed through our obedience**. Whether I was praying, serving, or simply being present, each act of obedience deepened my connection with God and enhanced my ability to support others through prayer.

REFLECTIVE QUESTIONS

1. How do you perceive the relationship between immediate prayer responses and their larger spiritual implications?
2. In what ways have you experienced or could you listen more attentively to divine instructions during prayer?
3. Can you identify a time when your prayer focus shifted significantly? What prompted this change, and what was the outcome?
4. Reflect on a situation where you felt your prayers were unanswered. How might this perspective shift if you considered a broader divine purpose?
5. How does the concept of spiritual warfare over destinies challenge or affirm your current understanding of prayer's role in your life?

ACTIONABLE STEPS

- **Cultivate a Responsive Prayer Life**: Begin by setting aside time daily to not only speak but listen during prayer, staying open to new directions or burdens the Holy Spirit may impart.
- **Equip Yourself with Scripture and Prophecy**: Regularly study and meditate on the Scriptures and

any prophetic words you have received, using them as tools in your prayer and daily decisions.

- **Engage in Community Intercession**: Join or initiate a prayer group focused on interceding for others' destinies and supporting each other through shared spiritual battles, enhancing your collective impact on the kingdom.

JOURNALING **Prompt**

Reflect on the phrase "Contend for the destinies" from Chapter 27. How does this call to action resonate with your current spiritual journey? Write about a destiny (either personal or someone else's) you feel led to pray for and any steps you are inspired to take in this intercessory journey.

∾

CHAPTER 28

TIMES AND SEASONS

Your prayers are a vital part of God's unfolding plans. Whether short-lived or spanning a lifetime, each prayer you utter weaves into the larger tapestry of His purposes. Persist in your prayers, for through them, you participate in the divine narrative that shapes the world.

"Pray without ceasing." (1 Thessalonians 5:17, NKJV)

I n this chapter, I explore the diverse world of **prayer assignments** as described in the Bible. It's fascinating to see how each prayer assignment varies, from quick, one-time prayers to commitments that last a lifetime. More importantly, it's not just about learning these stories; it's about actively participating in prayer, ensuring we don't miss the chance to collaborate with God.

Prayer assignments come in all shapes and sizes. Some require just a moment of our time, while others call for persistent, ongoing intercession. This variety teaches us to remain flexible and receptive to what the Holy Spirit might prompt us to do, rather than just sticking to what we've done before or what we've heard others do.

Take Abram's dialogue with God about Sodom and Gomorrah, for example. This might have been a short discussion, but it was deeply significant. It teaches us about the potential impact of our prayers and the importance of our **connection with God** in influencing big decisions.

Moses's story is quite different. His entire life was an **intercessory mission for Israel.** From his experience, we learn about the possibility and necessity of lifelong commitments in our prayer lives. Despite the Israelites' repeated failures, like creating the golden calf or doubting God's promises, Moses continuously stood before God to plead for mercy on their behalf.

Then there's Samuel, who promised to keep praying for Israel even after they chose to have a king, which wasn't God's ideal plan. His steadfast dedication reminds us that our commitment to pray for others should be based on our **obedience to God**, not dependent on how people treat us or whether they know about our prayers.

Ezra, too, had a critical prayer role. When he led the Jews back to Jerusalem, he found them repeating the sins that had led to their exile. His prayers were part of his larger duty to lead and teach the people according to **God's laws.**

Daniel's prayer life is another profound example. His commitment to daily prayers influenced not only his personal circumstances but also the broader political and spiritual realms. His story shows us the power of consistent, **strategic prayer** and its place in fulfilling God's larger purposes.

Lastly, consider Anna and Simeon, whose life's work was praying for the Messiah's arrival. Their dedication shows that focused, expectant prayer is powerful and that God honors such commitment, as they both witnessed when they met the infant Jesus.

These stories highlight the various prayer assignments we might encounter. Whether our calling involves a brief prayer or a lifelong mission, each prayer plays a crucial role in **God's plan**.

REFLECTIVE QUESTIONS

1. How do you adapt your prayer strategy according to the duration and intensity required by different prayer assignments?
2. What can you learn from Abram's negotiation with God about being bold in your prayers?
3. In what ways can you incorporate consistent prayer into your daily life, similar to Moses and Daniel?
4. How can Samuel's and Ezra's examples inspire you to pray for your community or nation, regardless of their response or awareness of your prayers?
5. What specific prayer assignment do you feel called to commit to, and how can you prepare for its long-term demands?

ACTIONABLE STEPS

- **Cultivate Flexibility in Prayer**: Develop an adaptable prayer routine that allows you to respond to different types of prayer needs as they arise, whether they are brief or require prolonged intercession.
- **Equip Yourself with Biblical Examples**: Regularly study biblical figures who exemplified effective prayer lives. Use their stories as a model for

developing your own strategic and impactful prayer practices.

- **Engage in Focused Prayer Assignments**: Identify a specific area or cause for which you can consistently pray, much like Anna and Simeon. Commit to this focus, and organize your prayer life around this central theme.

Journaling **Prompt**

Reflect on a past prayer assignment that you feel was particularly impactful. What were the circumstances, and how did you see God move? Consider how this experience can inform and inspire your current and future prayer engagements.

~

CHAPTER 29

THE SOVIET UNION

Remember, your prayers have the power to affect monumental changes, not just in individual lives but across nations and history. Never underestimate the role you play in God's sovereign plan through prayer.

"The earnest prayer of a righteous person has great power and produces wonderful results." (James 5:16b, NKJV)

In this chapter, I want to share the powerful story of how **Spirit-directed prayer** played a crucial role in one of the 20th century's most significant geopolitical events—the fall of the Soviet Union. This story is a strong reminder of the profound impact that focused, collective prayer can have on the world.

The Soviet Union was a major force globally from 1922 to 1991. For the younger readers who might not recognize its outline on a map, it was a union of 15 countries under a strict communist regime where religious freedom was almost entirely suppressed, except in state-controlled churches.

During a tourist mission in these challenging conditions, I saw firsthand the oppressive effects of communism—long lines for basic necessities, a noticeable fear among the people, and a general lack of freedom. However, amidst this repression, I encountered the underground church. Despite the risk of severe punishment, the believers' faces radiated joy and peace—a stark contrast to the fear and control evident on the streets. This encounter showed me that **faith could flourish** even under the most oppressive regimes.

What's truly remarkable is that the Soviet Union didn't end due to a war or violent uprising but through the **persistent prayers of people** around the world, including a group I was fortunate to be part of. We believed deeply in the power of prayer to bring about change, and this belief was profound. Under the guidance of Kenneth E. Hagin, we learned to pray with precision, using Scriptures to guide our intercessions for the nations. This structured approach helped us to understand God's heart for the nations and align our prayers accordingly.

One of the key aspects of our prayer meetings involved using specific biblical passages that emphasized the importance of waiting on God's timing and the powerful outcomes of righteous prayer. Scriptures like James 5:7 and 5:16b, Zechariah 10:1, and Hosea 6:3 encouraged us to pray for **spiritual rain to bring about a harvest of souls** and transformation within the nations.

Over time, our group evolved from simply reciting prayers to engaging deeply in spiritual communication. We prayed in tongues, allowing the Holy Spirit to intercede through us. This deep, spiritual engagement was crucial because our prayers went beyond our own understanding—we were engaging in a spiritual battle for the hearts and minds of millions and influencing the **spiritual climate of a global superpower.**

The results were nothing short of miraculous. No single human action could claim credit for the changes that occurred.

Instead, the transformation of the Soviet Union was a clear testament to God's power working through the faithful prayers of His people. Leaders changed, policies shifted, and the entire communist system eventually collapsed, leading to new freedoms and the spread of the gospel across the region.

To conclude, the fall of the Soviet Union is a powerful testament to the effectiveness of prayer. It challenges us to consider how we might contribute to significant changes in our world through our prayers today. Whether we are praying for nations, leaders, or global issues, our prayers are impactful. They extend beyond our own lives and can shape history in ways that we might only fully understand in hindsight.

REFLECTIVE QUESTIONS

1. How can understanding the historical context of the Soviet Union help us appreciate the scale of its transformation through prayer?
2. In what ways does the suppression of religion impact a society, and how can prayer combat these effects?
3. Reflect on a time when you witnessed or experienced the power of hidden or suppressed communities (like the underground church) coming to light. What emotions and thoughts did this evoke?
4. What can be learned from the structured, scriptural approach to prayer taught by Kenneth E. Hagin?
5. How does the story of Mikhail Gorbachev inspire you to believe in the possibility of change in seemingly rigid systems or leaders?

- **Cultivate a Historical Perspective**: Take time to learn about the history and political climates of countries or regions you are praying for. Understanding their past can enrich your prayer life and increase your empathy and effectiveness in prayer.
- **Equip Yourself with Scriptural Promises**: Integrate specific scriptures into your daily prayers, especially those that promise divine intervention and change. This will ground your prayers in biblical truth and power.
- **Engage in Global Intercessory Prayer**: Actively participate in or form prayer groups focused on international issues. Use the power of collective prayer to seek spiritual breakthroughs in areas of the world that are experiencing conflict, oppression, or transformation.

JOURNALING **Prompt**

Reflect on the concept of "Spirit-directed prayer" discussed in Chapter 29. How does this idea influence your understanding of prayer's role in societal and global changes? Consider a specific area or issue in the world today where you feel led to direct such prayer.

~

Harrison House is a Spirit-filled, Word of Faith Christian publisher dedicated to spreading the message of faith, hope, and love through our wide range of inspiring publications. Committed to the messages that highlight the power of the Word and Spirit, we provide books, devotionals, and study guides that empower believers to live victorious, faith-filled lives.

Our resources are designed to help readers grow spiritually, strengthen their faith, and experience the transformative power of God's Word. Harrison House is passionate about equipping Christians with the tools they need to fulfill their divine purpose and impact the world for Christ.

www.ingramcontent.com/pod-product-compliance
Lightning Source LLC
Chambersburg PA
CBHW070036100426
42740CB00013B/2701